SABRINA FISHER REECE

BALANCE

And Why We Need It

Copyright © 2026 by SaBrina Fisher Reece

All rights reserved. No part of this publication may be reproduced, stored, or transmitted in any form or by any means, electronic, mechanical, photocopying, recording, scanning, or otherwise without written permission from the publisher. It is illegal to copy this book, post it to a website, or distribute it by any other means without permission.

SaBrina Fisher Reece asserts the moral right to be identified as the author of this work.

Designations used by companies to distinguish their products are often claimed as trademarks. All brand names and product names used in this book and on its cover are trade names, service marks, trademarks, and registered trademarks of their respective owners. The publishers and the book are not associated with any product or vendor mentioned in this book. None of the companies referenced within the book have endorsed the book.

First edition

This book was professionally typeset on Reedsy. Find out more at reedsy.com

This book is dedicated to every person who has felt pulled in too many directions and quietly wondered how to find their center again. May these pages remind you that balance is not weakness, but wisdom. May you learn to steady your thoughts, honor your emotions, and walk through life grounded, aware, and whole.
−Bri Reece

Contents

Preface	ii
1 Why Do We Need Balance	1
2 Male vs Female Energy	18
3 Balance with Food	27
4 Emotional Balance	33
5 Finding Balance Through Peace	44
6 Loving Me Again	51
7 Being Balanced Emotionally	65
8 Daily Practices to Help You Achieve Balance	71
9 Everyday Alignment	78
10 Returning to My True Nature	85
About the Author	97
Also by SaBrina Fisher Reece	100

Preface

This book is for those who have reached a quiet understanding about life that no longer needs defending. You no longer feel compelled to explain what you sense or argue what you know in your spirit. You simply recognize that there is more happening beneath the surface of everyday life than what we can physically see. You understand now that being human is not separate from being spiritual, and that both exist together, shaping how we experience the world.

This book is written for those who have started to sense that more is happening beneath the surface of their daily lives than they were ever taught to notice. Thoughts influence emotions. Emotions influence decisions. Decisions shape outcomes. Even when we cannot see it, energy moves through every part of our experience. Love cannot be physically touched, fear cannot be placed on a table and examined, and faith cannot be measured with an instrument, yet each one directs behavior in ways that are undeniable. Every day we respond to internal forces that quietly shape what we say, how we react, and what we believe is possible.

Awareness of this connection rarely arrives in one dramatic moment. It develops over time. Life experiences have a way of pushing us to look deeper. Loss can do it. Disappointment can do it. Reflection can do it. There are seasons when logic alone cannot explain the weight we feel or the relief we experience.

Gradually, many of us begin to recognize that our internal condition and our external circumstances are not separate. When our thoughts feel scattered and our emotions feel unstable, life appears chaotic. When we experience even brief moments of inner steadiness, situations that once felt overwhelming become manageable.

The purpose of this book is to explore why balance is not optional but necessary. Mind, body, and energy operate as one system, and when one area is neglected, the strain shows up somewhere else. Stress settles into muscles. Unprocessed emotion surfaces in relationships. Constant mental pressure drains physical strength. Disconnection from yourself creates tension in places you cannot immediately name. Imbalance does not always announce itself loudly, but it reveals itself through fatigue, irritability, confusion, and a lingering sense that something is off.

Restoring balance does not require dramatic life changes or denial of reality. It begins internally. Shifts in awareness lead to shifts in response. When your inner state becomes steadier, the world around you may not instantly transform, but your experience of it does. You respond with more clarity. You pause before reacting. You choose with greater intention.

Balance is often misunderstood as perfection or constant positivity. That is not what this book is about. Pain exists. Pressure exists. Conflict exists. The goal is not to pretend those realities disappear. The goal is to develop the strength to hold opposing forces without falling apart. Strength and vulnerability can exist in the same person. Logic and intuition can guide decisions together. Action and rest both have their place. Balance is the ability to live in that tension without being consumed by it.

Life will continue to pull you in many different directions. Responsibilities will compete for your attention. Emotions will rise unexpectedly. Circumstances will shift regularly. Learning how to return to your center in the middle of that movement is what creates stability. Balance is not avoidance. It is alignment. It is the practice of coming back to yourself again and again, no matter what is happening around you.

This book was written for real people living real lives. People with responsibilities, emotions, questions, and a desire to feel more grounded and whole. You do not need to follow a specific belief system or consider yourself spiritually advanced to benefit from this book. You only need openness. Openness to understanding yourself more deeply. Openness to the idea that balance is something you can cultivate, not something you have to chase.

If you are reading this, you are already becoming more aware. This book is not here to tell you who to be. It is here to help you listen more closely to yourself and understand why balance is not optional, but essential.

Welcome to **BALANCE: and why we need it**.

1

Why Do We Need Balance

Balance is not the reward at the end of life. It is the way you choose to walk through it. Life is truly a gift. Once we all realize that we can determine the quality of our lives by how we chose to live, then mankind will understand that it's a wonderful gift to have the ability to design the life that you desire. I know horrible things happen at times and that makes it harder to believe that you have any control over your life, but you do.

No you can not force your will onto others. Yes, many situations and circumstances seem to bee unavoidable but how we choose to proceed afterwards is completely up to us. I could have totally given up on life after the horrific things I had been through. I could have ended up on drugs or taken my own life. I am so glad that even after years of suffering I did not give up. If you are reading this and you have thought about giving up many times, but you did not. I am so very proud of you.

I wish I could heal your pain. I wish I would have had someone to help me heal mine but the only person that can initiate healing for you, is you. You have to get up and take the reins. You have to want a better quality of life for yourself. Happiness, Love, great health, peace and prosperity are available to you. You are a limitless being who deserves all that the beautiful world has to offer.

For a long time, I thought balance was something I would eventually arrive at. That one day, after I healed enough, learned enough, grew enough, prayed enough, or worked enough, life would finally feel steady. That I would wake up and think, *Okay, I've got it now.* But that day never came, because balance was never meant to be a destination.

Balance is the journey itself. You choose balance each and ever day. We make balanced choices in our lives daily for example:

Balance shows up in ways so ordinary that we often don't even realize we are practicing it. Most of us are making decisions about balance every day of our lives without labeling them as spiritual or intentional. They feel practical and normal. But they are the very foundation of how we stay regulated, healthy, and grounded in our lives.

Think about something as simple as caring for a child. If your child has a cough and you give them one teaspoon of cough syrup, you are helping them. You are using wisdom. You are applying balance. But if you give them four teaspoons, you are no longer helping. Now you have a problem. Now you are rushing to the hospital. The medicine did not change. The intention did not change. What changed was the amount. That is balance. The same thing that heals can harm when taken without moderation and balance.

Food, which I speak about in dept in Chapter #3, is another easy example. I love cookies. Most of us do. If you eat one or two cookies and really enjoy them, you feel satisfied. You had a moment of pleasure. You didn't punish yourself for eating two cookies. But if you eat ten cookies in one sitting, you will probably wake up feeling sick, bloated, and disappointed in yourself. The cookie was not bad. Enjoying it was not wrong. The imbalance is what created the discomfort.

I enjoy a glass of wine. Sweet red wine is my favorite. One glass helps me relax. Two glasses might still be fine. But if I drink four, I feel disconnected from myself. I feel foggy and not in control. I feel like I made choices that weren't aligned with who I want to be. Nothing about the wine changed. What changed was my awareness of when enough became too much.

We are told to drink water, and we should. Our bodies need it. But doctors also remind us that drinking too much water can be dangerous. Even water, something essential to life, becomes harmful when taken without balance. That truth alone should tell us that moderation is not about restriction. It is about respect. Respect for the body. Respect for the mind. Respect for life itself.

I remember years ago watching my Aunt Sabra care for her daughter, who was disabled. One day I saw her mixing baking soda into a glass of water. She told me that a small amount can help with gas or an upset stomach. But she was clear that too much baking soda can seriously harm the body. That stayed with me. Even remedies require wisdom. Even solutions require limits.

We make these choices constantly. We balance rest and productivity. We balance social time and solitude. We balance spending and saving. We balance speaking and listening. We balance giving and receiving. When we ignore balance, life feels chaotic. When we honor it, life feels manageable.

Exercise is one of the clearest places where the importance of balance becomes obvious in everyday life. I love a man who takes care of his body. I completely respect discipline.

Taking responsibility for your health says something powerful about a person's character because it shows that they value their physical well being and understand that the body needs care in order to function well over the long term. Strength, endurance, and physical vitality require commitment, and there is something admirable about someone who makes the effort to stay active instead of allowing their health to deteriorate from neglect. Movement, training, and exercise are a huge part of my life because the body was designed to move, grow stronger, and remain capable as the years go by.

The problem begins when discipline quietly crosses the line into obsession. I can't stand gym rats, men who are obsessed with working out seven days a week as if their entire identity revolves around the next workout or the next muscle gain. That kind of relationship with exercise stops being about health and slowly becomes another form of control. Instead of caring for the body, the body begins to feel like something that must constantly be pushed, punished, or perfected. Hours that could be spent building relationships, enjoying life, or being present in the world start disappearing into endless workouts that are driven less by health and more by compulsion. A healthy body should support a full life rather than becoming the center of it. Balance allows strength without rigidity. Health without obsession. Exercise should make a person feel more alive, more energized, and more capable of participating in life rather than turning into something that dominates every waking moment.

Spirituality requires the same kind of balance. A deep connection to God or to a higher power can bring tremendous meaning, comfort, and guidance into a person's life. Faith has the ability to ground people in difficult moments, to remind them that life has purpose beyond the surface level of everyday struggles, and to help them live with compassion and humility. Loving God deeply and believing strongly in a higher power can become a powerful source of peace when that belief is integrated with the realities of living in the world. Spirituality should enhance a person's humanity rather than pulling them away from it.

Yet history and personal experience show what happens when spirituality loses that grounding. I have seen people become so consumed by religious ideas that they lose their ability to live a balanced life in the real world. Some individuals become so absorbed in spiritual identity that they withdraw from family, responsibilities, and the ordinary human connections that make life meaningful. Entire groups of people have been drawn into cults or extreme belief systems that separate them from their loved ones and convince them that isolation is a form of devotion. That kind of imbalance turns faith into something rigid and fearful instead of something compassionate and life giving. God does not ask us to abandon our humanity. God asks us to live it consciously. Faith should bring peace, love, clarity, and compassion. When it produces fear, extreme judgment, or emotional disconnection from others, something within that spiritual life has drifted out of balance.

Curiosity about the mysteries of the universe is another place where balance matters, even when the subject seems lighthearted or speculative. I enjoy a good alien movie and I have always believed that life beyond this planet probably exists in some form. The universe is far too vast and complex to assume that human beings are the only intelligent life that has ever emerged anywhere. That belief does not feel unreasonable to me, but I also recognize that believing something and becoming consumed by it are two completely different things. Curiosity can expand the imagination and make life interesting, yet curiosity can also become an endless rabbit hole if it is allowed to take over a person's thinking.

Because of that, I keep my belief about extraterrestrial life in what I call the entertainment box. It is an interesting idea to consider, something that can be explored through movies, documentaries, and conversations about the possibilities that exist beyond our planet. At the same time, there is very little that any individual person can actually do about whether aliens exist or what might be happening somewhere in the universe. If they do exist, there is nothing I can control about it and most of what humanity learns about such things will probably come through whatever information governments or scientific institutions decide to release. Spending hours obsessing over theories about what might be happening somewhere out in space would not improve the quality of my life here on Earth.

Life is happening right in front of us, and becoming overly consumed with distant possibilities can easily distract from the responsibility and opportunity of living fully in the present. Humans were placed on this planet for a reason. Maybe God put us here and put them somewhere else, and perhaps whatever exists on other planets is simply not our concern right now. There is a certain humility in accepting that not every mystery needs to be solved for us to live meaningful lives. Balance keeps curiosity healthy instead of consuming. Wonder can exist without obsession. Imagination can expand without pulling a person away from the life they are meant to live here and now.

What we begin to understand is that balance is not something we master once. It is something we practice daily. In how we eat, how we work, how we love, how we believe, how we rest.

Most people already recognize the feeling of excess before they have the language to describe it. The body notices first. You feel tension in your shoulders, fatigue in your chest, or a quiet heaviness in your stomach that tells you something is out of alignment. The mind begins to feel scattered or irritated. The spirit starts whispering that something about the way life is being lived is off center. Balance is not some abstract spiritual idea that only philosophers talk about. It is simply the ability to notice those signals and respond to them instead of ignoring them until life begins to crack under the pressure.

You can see this clearly in everyday relationships, especially in marriage. Imagine a husband who spends his entire day operating in work mode. He is solving problems, making decisions, carrying responsibility, and pushing through stress so he can provide for his family. That energy can be necessary and honorable in the workplace, but if he walks through the door still operating in that same mode, the home begins to feel like an extension of the job instead of a place of connection, love and peace. His children do not need a manager when he gets home. His wife does not need another authority figure walking through the house issuing instructions. What the family needs at that moment is a different side of him, the side that can soften, connect, laugh, listen, and become emotionally present again. The shift from worker to husband and father is not weakness. It is balance.

The same kind of shift exists on the other side of the relationship. Imagine a wife who has spent the entire day in caretaker mode. She has been organizing schedules, feeding children, cleaning messes, answering questions, and creating the structure that keeps a household functioning. That role carries its own form of leadership and responsibility. Yet if the day ends and she continues relating to her husband in the exact same way she relates to the children, the dynamic of the relationship begins to erode. A marriage cannot thrive when one partner feels like another person being managed or corrected. When a spouse returns home after carrying the weight of a long workday, what he hopes to encounter is not another authority figure or another person directing his every move. He hopes to feel welcomed, seen, and valued as a partner. The ability to step out of caretaker mode and step back into the role of loving spouse is another form of balance.

When those shifts stop happening, relationships quietly begin to suffocate. It does not happen all at once. It shows up slowly through frustration, distance, resentment, and the feeling that two people are living in the same house but no longer meeting each other where they are. Many marriages do not collapse because people stopped loving each other. They collapse because both people became trapped inside one mode of being and lost the flexibility to meet life and each other in different ways. A healthy relationship requires the ability to move between structure and connection, responsibility and presence, discipline and warmth.

This is why the conversation about masculine and feminine energies inside every person matters. Every human being carries the capacity for both structure and softness, leadership and receptivity, direction and emotional connection. The husband who works all day also carries the ability to come home and reconnect with the people he loves. The wife who creates structure for the family all day also carries the ability to shift back into partnership and intimacy with her husband. These are not rigid roles tied to gender. They are expressions of human balance.

Life constantly asks us to move between different ways of being. Work requires focus, discipline, and problem solving. Relationships require listening, patience, and emotional presence. Parenting requires guidance and protection, but also tenderness and encouragement. If someone becomes locked into only one way of showing up in the world, everything around them begins to feel strained. Balance is the ability to move between those states with awareness rather than getting stuck in one of them.

Balance is not about denying pleasure or stripping life of joy. It is about learning to recognize when something has crossed the line from healthy engagement into excess. It means enjoying what life offers without allowing enjoyment to slowly become self betrayal. It means being devoted to something without becoming so consumed by it that the rest of life begins to suffer. Discipline still exists, but it is no longer harsh or punishing. Strength still exists, but it is no longer expressed through force.

Living this way requires constant adjustment. There is no permanent formula that solves it forever. Each season of life brings new responsibilities, new pressures, and new opportunities to drift too far in one direction. Balance is the ongoing practice of noticing when that drift begins to happen and gently guiding yourself back toward center. It is the quiet awareness that life is always moving, relationships are always evolving, and the healthiest way to live within that movement is to stay flexible enough to respond rather than rigidly holding on to one way of being.

Balance: And Why We Need It was written to comfort people as they move through the process of becoming who they were put here to be. It is, without question, an ongoing journey of self-discovery, and while it isn't always easy, it is always worth it. How challenging or gentle that journey feels often depends on how willing you are to move with intention rather than resistance.

And yes, my youngest daughter's name happens to be Journey. That's not the reason I use the word so often, but there is something quietly poetic about it. Because balance doesn't arrive all at once. It unfolds step by step, moment by moment, mile by mile.

We've talked about emotional balance. We've explored masculine and feminine energy. We've touched on spiritual balance, nourishment, and the art of returning to center. But there are other forms of balance that quietly show up in our lives… One of the biggest is relationship balance.

Relationships are mirrors. They show us where we are aligned and where we are not. There is a reason the Bible speaks about being equally yoked. That does not mean identical. It means moving in the same direction. Carrying similar values and sharing a comparable sense of responsibility, growth, and commitment.

When relationships are imbalanced, one person pulls while the other resists. One grows while the other stays stagnant. One carries the emotional weight while the other coasts. Over time, that imbalance becomes exhausting.

Balance in relationships requires honesty. Not just with the other person, but with yourself. Are you over-giving to avoid abandonment? Are you over functioning to feel needed? Are you shrinking to keep peace? Are you staying silent to avoid conflict? Love should not cost you your center.

Healthy relationships allow space for individuality and togetherness at the same time. They allow strength and vulnerability to coexist. They allow growth without competition. When a relationship pulls you away from yourself instead of bringing you closer, something is out of alignment.

Another form of balance that people rarely talk about is the balance between doing and being. The culture we live in places enormous value on productivity. People are praised for how much they accomplish, how busy they are, and how many things they can manage at once. Work, effort, and achievement are treated as signs of value, while quiet moments of rest are often dismissed as laziness or wasted time. Many people grow up believing that rest has to be earned after enough work has been done, as if stillness only has value once exhaustion has already set in. What often gets overlooked is that being still is not the opposite of growth. In many cases, stillness is the place where growth actually begins. A quiet mind can hear things that a busy mind cannot. A rested body can respond to life with more clarity than one that is constantly pushing itself past its limits.

A life that revolves entirely around doing eventually pulls a person away from their inner life. When every day is filled with tasks, responsibilities, deadlines, and goals, it becomes easy to measure your worth by what you produce rather than who you are. The mind starts to believe that value comes only through output, and the moment you slow down a quiet sense of guilt begins to creep in. Rest can start to feel uncomfortable because it is mistaken for falling behind. I know this pattern well because I lived it for many years. It took thirty years for me to understand that something as simple as sitting outside in my backyard and allowing the sun to warm my face is not wasted time. Those quiet moments are healthy for the mind and the spirit. They create space for reflection, gratitude, and a deeper connection with life that constant activity can easily drown out.

Developing that understanding has made me deeply grateful for the role balance now plays in my life. Balance teaches a person that their value does not disappear simply because they are not producing something at every moment of the day. Human worth is not tied only to accomplishment. Being alive, present, and aware of the world around you carries its own kind of value that cannot be measured by productivity. Once that truth settles in, life begins to feel less like a race that must constantly be won and more like a journey that can actually be experienced along the way.

Ambition and peace can exist together when balance is present. A person can work toward goals and build something meaningful while still appreciating the life they already have. Wanting to grow does not have to come from dissatisfaction with the present moment. It is possible to be driven without feeling constantly drained or depleted. Building a future does not require ignoring the beauty of the present. A balanced life allows room for effort and enjoyment to exist side by side instead of competing with each other.

Time is another area where balance quietly shapes the quality of a person's life. The way someone spends their hours eventually becomes the way they spend their years. Every commitment, responsibility, and activity fills a portion of the limited time we have here, which means awareness about how that time is used becomes incredibly important. Balance with time requires learning when to move quickly and when to slow down. Some situations call for focused effort and decisive action, while others require patience and space to unfold naturally. A life where everything feels urgent eventually becomes exhausting because constant urgency removes the ability to appreciate what is happening in the present moment.

Understanding the rhythm of different seasons in life helps restore that balance with time. There are periods when building, working, and creating require more attention and energy. Other seasons call for maintaining what has already been built rather than constantly expanding. Some parts of life encourage solitude and reflection, while other periods invite connection, community, and shared experiences. Expecting life to move at the same pace forever creates unnecessary pressure because human life naturally moves through different phases. Accepting those changes allows a person to work hard when it is time to build and rest without guilt when it is time to slow down.

There is another kind of balance that often goes unnoticed. The balance between solitude and connection. Some people disappear into isolation and slowly lose their sense of belonging. Others stay constantly surrounded by people and gradually lose their sense of self. Neither extreme is healthy.

Being alone gives you space to think without outside noise. It allows you to sort through your thoughts and understand what you actually feel instead of reacting to everyone around you. Spending time with other people shows you where you truly stand. Relationships expose your strengths and your weaknesses. They reveal your patience level, your triggers, and your growth. Too much time alone can slowly turn into isolation. Too much time around people can drain you and leave you exhausted. Balance means knowing when to pull back and when to lean in without losing yourself in either direction.

The same principle applies to faith and effort. For a long time, I believed everything depended on how hard I worked. If I pushed enough, stayed disciplined enough, and refused to quit, I assumed things would eventually fall into place. That mindset carried me far, but it also wore me out. Eventually I realized that effort alone cannot control every outcome. There are moments when trust is necessary. There are seasons when you have to release the need to force results.

On the other hand, relying only on faith without taking action leads nowhere. Waiting for things to change without doing the work creates stagnation. Trying to control everything through effort creates tension. Real balance means showing up, doing your part, and then allowing space for what you cannot control.

Balance is knowing when to pray and when to act. When to release and when to step forward. When to trust the process and when to participate in it.

Another subtle but powerful balance is between speaking and listening. Some people speak to be heard but never listen to understand. Others listen endlessly but never speak their truth. Both are imbalanced. Your voice matters. So does your ability to hear.

Balance allows conversation instead of competition. Dialogue instead of domination. It allows wisdom to flow instead of ego to lead. There is also balance in how you hold your past. Some people live stuck in it, and others refuse to acknowledge it. Both steal peace from themselves.

Balance allows you to learn from your past without living there. To honor what shaped you without letting it define you. You can remember without reliving it over and over as I did.

Life will always contain responsibilities. Bills arrive whether we feel ready or not. Obligations exist in every direction. Families depend on us, work asks things from us, and commitments do not disappear simply because we feel tired or overwhelmed. Yet balance reminds us that joy is not something reserved for the distant future once every responsibility has finally been completed. Joy is part of the strength that helps us carry those responsibilities in the first place. Without it, life slowly turns into nothing more than survival. Joy gives the mind space to breathe and gives the heart a reason to keep moving forward. A person who allows joy to exist in the middle of ordinary life stays connected to hope, and that connection becomes the quiet fuel that keeps everything else functioning.

Waiting for the perfect moment to feel joy often means waiting forever. Life rarely lines up in a neat sequence where every problem is solved and every obligation disappears at the same time. Balance teaches us to welcome joy into ordinary days instead of postponing it until everything looks perfect. Simple moments often carry the most meaning if we are paying attention to them. One of the memories that always warms my heart is hearing my children laugh hysterically somewhere in the house. In those moments it does not matter what task I am working on or what responsibility is waiting for me. I stop, I listen, and I smile. The sound of their laughter reminds me that life is happening right now and not sometime later when everything finally settles down.

Balance does not remove hardship from life. Difficult moments still appear without warning and sometimes hit the nervous system before logic has time to respond. Financial pressure can still tighten the chest when an unexpected expense shows up. Stressful news can still create a rush of emotion before the mind has time to sort through it. Those reactions are human and completely normal. The difference now is that temporary stress no longer has permission to steal long term peace. The moment passes, the problem gets addressed, and life continues forward instead of spiraling into fear or exhaustion.

A hard day does not mean that growth has disappeared. Moments of frustration do not erase the progress that has been built over time. Losing patience once does not cancel the effort someone has made to become calmer and more grounded. Balance is not fragile and it does not vanish the moment a person stumbles. Real balance is something that can be returned to again and again. The ability to come back to center matters far more than never being shaken at all.

Every stage of life introduces new challenges that test that center. Financial strain, emotional setbacks, disappointment, health concerns, and tension in relationships are all part of the human experience. No one escapes those seasons entirely. The purpose of balance is not to avoid being shaken by life but to recognize when you have drifted away from your center and gently guide yourself back without shame. Learning how to return to that steady place changes the way you experience everything that comes your way.

Growth begins the moment awareness enters the situation. When you notice yourself spiraling into anxiety and choose to pause before reacting, balance is being practiced. When you accept that life will always include moments of ease alongside moments of discomfort without turning either one into a permanent identity, balance is being practiced. When you work through a problem while protecting your sense of peace instead of sacrificing it, balance is being practiced in a very real and practical way.

This way of living has very little to do with controlling every outcome that life delivers. Circumstances will change in ways that no one can fully predict or manage. What balance strengthens is the internal foundation that allows a person to remain steady even while the external world shifts around them. The relationship you build with yourself determines how stable you feel when life becomes uncertain. As that foundation grows stronger, the way you move through life begins to change. You reactions begin to soften. Recovery happens faster. Confidence in your own ability to handle life deepens.

Balance is not a destination where someone eventually arrives and stays forever. Life continues to move, and balance moves with it. The way you think, speak, respond, and recover from difficulty gradually reflects the steadiness you have built inside yourself. The more consistently you return to that center, the stronger and more resilient you become.

Resilience allows a person to live fully without being destroyed by the natural ups and downs that come with being human. Balance is what protects that resilience and keeps life from pulling you too far in any direction for too long. It allows responsibility and joy, effort and rest, strength and compassion to exist together in a healthy way.

Balance is not optional. It is necessary.

2

Male vs Female Energy

For most of my life, I was told I was "too much" of something I didn't even know how to name yet. To others I was too dominant and controlling. At work I was deemed too strong and direct. Too assertive and opinionated. To many throughout my life I was too confident and too independent. The negative way it was framed always came with a sting: *You're acting like a man.*

I heard that sentence more times than I can count, and every time I heard it, it carried the same underlying message. Something about me was wrong. Something about the way I moved through the world did not match what a woman was supposed to be. I was supposed to be sweet, soft-spoken, agreeable, nurturing, and accommodating. I was expected to dim myself, defer, and wait on the advice of others. Instead, I was leading the charge, deciding, building, and taking responsibility. I was running businesses and managing people. I was making hard calls and final decision. I was holding things together for my kids and I, and I was doing it unapologetically because I had no choice. My life required it.

What I did not understand then, but I do understand deeply

now, is that what people were reacting to was not me being too strong for a woman or too dominant for their comfort. What they were sensing was my energy. Masculine and feminine energy are not social roles or personality labels. They are spiritual forces that exist within every human being. They are how creation moves, how ideas become form, how intention turns into action. We all carry both. We always have and we always will.

Masculine energy is the part of us that organizes life. It builds structure, creates direction, makes decisions, and protects what matters. It is the steady force that plans, moves things forward, and holds a boundary when something needs to be protected or completed. Feminine energy moves differently. It is the part of us that feels deeply, senses what is happening beneath the surface, imagines new possibilities, nurtures growth, and allows life to flow rather than forcing it. It listens before acting. It receives before responding. Both of these energies exist to support life in different ways, and neither one is greater or lesser than the other. When they are working together, they create balance. When one is pushed aside, misunderstood, or overused, something inside us eventually begins to feel strained. The body feels it. The mind feels it and most importantly the spirit feels it.

For a long time I believed something about me was wrong. I was told in many ways that parts of my personality were flaws that needed to be corrected. What I eventually came to understand is that what I was living was not a flaw at all. It was survival. I had learned to rely heavily on one type of energy because it was the only way I knew how to keep moving through life. When life demands that you constantly be strong, responsible, productive, or protective, you begin to live mostly from the structured, doing side of yourself. The problem is not that this energy exists. The problem is when a person is never allowed to soften into the other side of their nature. When there is no room to rest, to feel, to receive, or to trust intuition, the inner balance that human beings are designed to live with slowly disappears.

Every human being carries both masculine and feminine energetic qualities within them. This has nothing to do with the physical body someone was born with. It has nothing to do with sexual organs or gender roles that society assigns. We are talking about internal energies that shape how we think, act, feel, and respond to life. The masculine aspect within us gives us the ability to build, protect, decide, and move forward with clarity. The feminine aspect within us gives us the ability to feel, create, connect, and understand what cannot always be explained logically. One energy directs movement. The other senses where movement should go. One builds structure. The other brings life and meaning into that structure.

When these two energies are allowed to exist together inside a person, something powerful happens. The mind becomes clearer because logic and intuition are both being used. Decisions become wiser because they are not driven only by pressure or only by emotion. Strength no longer feels like constant tension, and softness no longer feels like weakness. They begin to support each other instead of competing with each other.

The imbalance many people experience in life is not because they lack one of these energies. It is because somewhere along the way they were taught to distrust or suppress one side of themselves. Some people are conditioned to live only through structure, productivity, and control, leaving little room for creativity, emotion, or rest. Others are taught to stay in feeling and intuition without learning how to create structure that supports their visions. Neither extreme brings peace. Harmony happens when the parts of us that build and the parts of us that feel are allowed to work together instead of canceling each other out.

This balance is not something we achieve once and then keep forever. It is something we return to again and again as we grow. Some seasons of life require more structure and action. Other seasons require more reflection, healing, and creativity. The goal is not to eliminate one energy in favor of the other. The goal is learning how to let both exist within us so that our lives are guided by strength and wisdom at the same time.

The real work of Balance is not choosing one energy over the other. It is learning when to lead and when to allow. When to push and when to soften. It is knowing when to take charge and when to surrender. Strength without softness becomes rigid and softness without strength becomes unstable. But when masculine and feminine energy are allowed to cooperate within you, life begins to flow differently. Decisions become clearer. Boundaries feel natural. Rest no longer feels like failure, and confidence no longer needs to prove itself. That is not gender politics. That is spiritual alignment.

For a long time, I internalized that criticism. I wondered if I was broken in some way. If I was missing something essential to womanhood. If being only five feet two meant I was supposed to compensate by being quieter, smaller, less commanding. I questioned whether I had somehow failed at femininity, as if femininity were a narrow script that everyone else had received except me. I looked like a cute little feminine young woman on the outside, but inside I was a lion in the wild trying to survive in the world alone.

It wasn't until much later in life that I began to understand the truth. Masculine and feminine energy are not about gender. They are not about anatomy, hormones, or the roles society assigns us. They are energetic principles that exist within every human being. We all carry both. Always have. Always will.

Masculine energy shows up as action, structure, logic, protection, and direction. Feminine energy shows up as intuition, creativity, emotion, nurturing, and flow. Neither is better than the other. Neither is weak. Neither is dominant by design. They are meant to work together. When they are balanced, life feels steady, clear, and aligned. When they are out of balance, we feel scattered, reactive, exhausted, or disconnected from ourselves.

This is not abstract or mystical theory. This is practical knowledge you can apply to your everyday life. You can see it in how you make decisions, how you communicate, how you love, how you work, and how you respond to stress. When you are too far in one direction, either overly rigid or overly emotional, something inside you feels off. Balance restores harmony. Balance is the key to a happy and fulfilling life.

Once I understood this, I stopped trying to label myself or others and started paying attention to energy instead. I learned that true strength is not about suppressing one side of yourself but integrating both. This is not esoteric knowledge meant only for spiritual circles. This is real-world wisdom you can take to the bank, because when your internal energies are aligned, your external life follows.

Masculine energy is often associated with action, direction, logic, structure, protection, and leadership. Feminine energy is often associated with intuition, receptivity, creativity, emotion, nurturing, and flow. Neither is superior. Neither is complete on its own. They are meant to work together, not compete with each other. Problems arise when we are taught that one is acceptable for us and the other is not.

When a woman is told she must only embody softness, she is cut off from her power. When a man is told he must only embody strength, he is cut off from his heart. Both are incomplete expressions of the human experience. Balance does not mean choosing one energy over the other. Balance means learning how to integrate both in a way that feels authentic, aligned, and whole.

This misunderstanding is deeply rooted in how we talk about God. For centuries, we have used male language to describe the divine, not because God is male, but because language is limited and culture shaped the metaphors we used. God is not a man in the human sense of the word. God is an omnipotent, infinite energy that encompasses everything and everybody. Creation itself is the ultimate act of both masculine and feminine expression. There is intention and structure, which reflects masculine energy, and there is birth, creativity, and flow, which reflects feminine energy. To suggest that the source of all life embodies only one side of that spectrum is to misunderstand the nature of creation itself.

We are told that we were created in the image of God. Not men only. Not women only. But all of us. That means the full spectrum of energy exists within each person. The capacity to lead and the capacity to nurture. The ability we have to act and the ability we have to receive. Humans have the strength to build and the wisdom to feel. When we deny parts of ourselves in order to fit into rigid roles, we move out of alignment not just with ourselves, but with the very design of our being.

For years, I lived heavily in my masculine energy. I had to. I was responsible for livelihoods and outcomes. I had to make decisions that affected real people in real ways. I was decisive, strategic, and structured. I was strong because the world demanded strength from me. There is nothing wrong with that. Somebody had to do it. I'm glad I was able to. What was missing was not femininity, but permission. Permission to rest and receive. Permission to soften without feeling weak. I needed to learn to be emotionally present with myself instead of always pushing forward. But pushing forward was all that I knew.

Masculine energy unchecked can become rigid, controlling, and exhausting. Feminine energy suppressed can turn into resentment, emotional burnout, and disconnection from self. I learned this the hard way. Strength without softness eventually leads to imbalance, just as softness without structure can lead to instability. Balance is not about erasing who you are. It is about expanding who you allow yourself to be.

The most profound shift in my life came when I stopped trying to label myself as either masculine or feminine and started asking a better question. What does this moment require of me? Sometimes life requires action, boundaries, and leadership. Other times it requires patience, compassion, and surrender. Wisdom is knowing the difference. Balance is having access to both.

This is where many people get stuck. They believe that embodying one energy means betraying the other. They think that strength negates softness. Or that emotion weakens authority. Intuition does not undermine logic. In truth, the most grounded people are those who can move fluidly between energies without losing themselves. They know when to stand firm and when to yield. When you are spiritually aligned you know when to speak and when to listen. You sense when to push forward and when to pull inward.

As women, many of us were taught to fear our power. We were warned that being too strong would make us undesirable. Being too independent would make us intimidating. Too confident would make us lonely. So we learned to perform femininity instead of embodying it. We learned to soften our voices, second-guess our instincts, and downplay our accomplishments. That performance is not balance. It is suppression, which can lead to emotional imbalance.

True feminine energy is not weakness. It is depth, intuition and emotional intelligence. It the ability to sense what is unspoken and respond with wisdom. True masculine energy is not dominance. It is stability and strong presence. It is the ability to hold space and provide direction when needed. When these energies work together within us, we feel whole and grounded instead of fractured.

For men, the imbalance shows up differently but just as painfully. Many men were taught to suppress emotion, vulnerability, and tenderness. They were told that sensitivity was a liability, and feelings were a distraction. They were taught that intuition was irrational. In cutting themselves off from their feminine energy, they were taught to live disconnected from a large part of their humanity. Balance restores what was taken from both sides.

Understanding masculine and feminine energy is not about labeling yourself or placing yourself in a box. It is about liberation, about reclaiming the full range of who you are without apology. It is the realization that strength and softness can coexist within the same body, in the same moment, and even in the same decision. Each of us carries both masculine and feminine energy within us. The work is not in denying one or favoring the other, but in learning how to balance them together as one cohesive, positive force, an inner alignment that works in your favor rather than against you.

When I finally stopped apologizing for my leadership and stopped shaming myself for my sensitivity, something shifted. I no longer felt like I had to choose between being powerful and being gentle. I realized I was both. Always had been. Many of you can relate to this. The imbalance was never in me. It was in the expectations placed upon me.

This chapter is an invitation to release those expectations. To stop asking whether you are too much or not enough. To stop forcing yourself into one energy at the expense of the other. You were never meant to be half of yourself. You were meant to be whole.

Balance begins with understanding. Understanding that your assertiveness does not make you masculine in a way that negates your femininity. Your emotional depth does not make you weak. Whether you are a male or a female please understand that the divine within you is expansive, inclusive, and complete.

When you honor both energies within you, everything changes. You move through the world with confidence and compassion. You accept yourself without apology and set boundaries without guilt. You allow yourself to receive without fear. You act with intention instead of force and you rest when needed without shame. This is balance and alignment.

Alignment does not ask you to become someone new. It asks you to return to who you have always been. To come home to yourself.

3

Balance with Food

Food is energy. Not just calories or numbers on a label. Food is information. Food is frequency. Food carries intention, emotion, memory, and meaning. There is balance required as well when it comes to food. The mindset you are in when you take food into your body matters just as much as what is on the plate.

I refuse to live in a constant state of guilt around food. I love food and refuse to be one of those people who punishes themselves every time they eat a hamburger. I will not sit at a table and say things like, "I know I shouldn't have this," while taking a bite. I will absolutely not call myself names while chewing, turn one of life's greatest pleasures into a source of shame.

I enjoy food. I love fine dining. One of my dreams is to travel the world and experience food in different countries, different cultures, different kitchens. That is not indulgence to me. That is enjoying my life. That is happiness. That is nourishment on more than one level.

I am very intentional about the words I use around food and my body. Words are energy, a the body listens. The very cells that we are made of are intelligent and alive and they are always listening. So when we continuously belittle ourselves with insults and negative convictions, the very fiber of our being conforms to our own image of who we believe we are.

If we tell ourselves that we are stupid, fat and lazy and will never lose weight then the intelligent force that drives us conforms to just that. I was the one telling myself that I was broken, unwanted and unlovable. Most of the people in my life were unaware of my past trauma so I kept that story hidden from others while tormenting myself with it daily. It was me who reminded myself of my past. It was me who said, "I'm damaged goods." I chose to replay the hurtful day in my head over and over. Our words create our reality. Even if we never speak them aloud, we say them internally to ourselves which is just as damaging, if not more-so.

I have absolutely gained a significant amount of weight in my fifties. I do believe in working out to feel good and maintain optimal health. But all of those decisions must come from a place of balance. If you like exercise, incorporate it into your life in a healthy balanced way. Not in a self deprecating obsessive way.

When people sit down to eat while insulting themselves, shaming themselves, or speaking negatively over their bodies, that energy enters the food. You are not just digesting what's on the plate. You are digesting the emotion attached to it.

People call themselves fat casually. They criticize themselves constantly. They eat while mentally punishing themselves. Then they wonder why food feels heavy, why their relationship with their body feels adversarial, why eating never brings satisfaction.

I refuse to live that way. I don't think anyone else should

either. yes a balanced degree of exercise and eating healthy is a positive thing. But do it with the energy of love. Self-love, because we were put here to create heaven on earth for ourselves. Something as significant as food should be a happy, pleasurable experience.

This does not mean I ignore nutritional facts. It does not mean I am anti-health or anti-discipline. I fully support anyone who is on a weight-loss journey, especially when it is done with care, education, and self-respect. But what I will not support is a culture that turns the body into an enemy and food into a battleground.

We are living in a time where people are so desperate to lose weight that they are risking their health, their freedom, and sometimes their lives to do it. Weight-loss drugs originally created to treat diabetes have exploded in popularity. An estimated **one in eight adults in the United States has taken a GLP-1 weight-loss medication** like Ozempic or Wegovy . Thousands of emergency room visits have been linked to side effects like dehydration, severe gastrointestinal distress, and pancreatitis .

At the same time, people are purchasing counterfeit or unregulated versions of these drugs online or through underground markets, putting themselves at serious risk. All of this to shrink a body that was never meant to be hated into submission.

Weight-loss surgery tells a similar story. While bariatric surgery can be life-saving for some, research shows that many patients already struggle with depression and emotional distress before surgery, and some continue to struggle psychologically long after the weight is gone . Changing the body without addressing the mind and spirit does not guarantee peace.

That is why this chapter is not about restriction. It is about nourishment.

True nourishment asks a different question. Not "How do I punish my body into compliance?" but "How do I support my body with respect?"

I work out. Absolutely I do. I love my Zumba class. I believe in movement for good circulation. I believe in strength. I have a home gym. I call it the **Just Breathe Baby** home gym, and it is lime green, because joy matters even in discipline. But I refuse to let exercise become another reason to shame myself.

I set an intention to work out twice a week. That is my agreement with myself. If I work out once, I refuse to feel bad. If I miss a week, I do not spiral into self-criticism. I do not talk down to myself. I do not make movement transactional. I return to it when my body is ready.

Restriction culture teaches people that worth is earned through suffering. Balance teaches something very different. Balance teaches consistency over cruelty. Compassion over control and sustainability over extremes.

Globally, nearly **2.5 billion adults are overweight**, including almost **890 million living with obesity**. But what rarely gets discussed is the emotional cost of living in a body that society constantly criticizes. Research shows that obesity is strongly associated with **low self-esteem, anxiety, and depression**, largely because of stigma and shame, not just health factors . Up to **60 percent of people living with obesity experience psychiatric conditions**, including depression .

That tells me something important. The problem is not just weight. The problem is how people feel about themselves while carrying it.

When people hate their bodies, they disconnect from them. When they disconnect from their bodies, they stop listening.

When they stop listening, they make decisions rooted in desperation instead of wisdom.

Nourishment brings you back into relationship with yourself. When I sit down to eat, I set an intention. I choose to enjoy my food. I choose to be present in the moment and to speak kindly to myself. I choose to remember that my body is not my enemy. It is my partner. It has carried me through grief, childbirth, stress, surgery, trauma, joy, and survival. It deserves respect.

That does not mean I eat without awareness. It means I eat without punishment. There is a spiritual cost to constant restriction. When food becomes moralized, people start believing they are good or bad based on what they eat. That thinking spills into every area of life. It creates shame cycles that are incredibly hard to break.

Extreme restriction also fuels eating disorders, which carry some of the highest mortality rates of any mental health condition. Anorexia nervosa, in particular, has one of the highest death rates among psychiatric illnesses. This is not about vanity. This is about survival.

Balance does not live at the extremes. Balance lives in awareness. In moderation. In intention. In listening. In forgiveness. In nourishment. Food should not be something you fear. It should be something that supports your life. Movement should not be something you dread. It should be something that connects you to your body. Health should not be something you chase through punishment. It should be something you cultivate through care.

I want a life where I enjoy my meals. Where I savor flavor. I travel and taste and experience. Where I move my body because I love it, not because I hate it. Where my spiritual practice includes how I speak to myself when I look in the mirror and when I sit at the table. That is balance.

If you are on a weight-loss journey, I honor you. If you are healing your relationship with food, I see you. If you are learning to move your body without shame, I support you. if you are tired of living under the pressure of perfection, I invite you to rest here.

Nourishment over restriction is not about letting go of responsibility. It is about letting go of violence toward yourself.

Food is energy. Choose the kind that feeds your body, mind and spirit.

That is *Balance.*

4

Emotional Balance

Spiritual work is not something you complete and check off a list. It is not a phase you go through. It is not seasonal. It is a lifelong relationship with yourself. It is a learned behavior that should carry you through the rest of your life. I don't say that to discourage you or make it seem overwhelming. I say it because once you understand this, you stop judging yourself for still being human.

Total evolution does not mean you never feel pain again. It means you become aware enough to walk through pain without destroying yourself or others. You learn how to hold your emotions instead of letting them hold you hostage.

Emotional awareness is some of the deepest spiritual work you will ever do. Every single day, you are presented with choices. How do you respond.? How you regulate your emotions? How do you maintain balance and breathe through it? Happiness is not something that happens to you. You create it for yourself. These are daily decisions you make, sometimes minute by minute.

There are things in life that trigger emotions before you even have time to think. When I was younger I reacted to, a look, a harsh word, a driver in traffic. Sometimes your body reacts before your mind catches up. That is where true balance work begins. In that pause. In taking those few seconds to breathe. In that moment where you remember that you have a choice.

When I was younger, I did not know that I had any control over my emotions. I had a temper. A real one... I was not just astrologically a Lion, I was truly a fierce lion running around town with un-diagnosed PTST and a whole lot of pain inside. I had been through a lot in life, and I was angry about it. I was angry at people and circumstances. I was mad as hell at God. I felt like I had not been protected.

I did not understand that emotions were something I could work with. I thought they were something that happened to me just like all my past trauma, and I did not know I had and control. I definitely did not have any tools at that time. I didn't know there were options, or any way to release the pain I felt.

So I exploded. I screamed. I hollered. I acted a fool. I let raw emotion run wild. Untamed, unchecked and unfiltered. At the time, it felt justified. When you have pain that deep, expression feels like survival. The world is your enemy. But what I did not understand back then was that unregulated emotion does not heal pain. It multiplies it.

As time went on, life taught me some very hard lessons. No matter what you are feeling, no matter how justified the emotion seems, if you do not learn how to pause and regulate, you can destroy your life in a single moment. You can end up in jail or dead. You can hurt someone you love or ruin something that took years to build, all for one emotional explosion that lasted seconds.

That is not spiritual. That is survival without balance. One of the most significant lessons I have learned about emotions is this. No matter how unbearable they feel in the moment, they will pass. That does not minimize pain. It honors reality. If may not feel like it but the tight grip of pain loosens. Grief slowly shifts and fear softens. The next day is often just a little lighter. And the next day, a little lighter still.

When you are in the middle of emotional pain, it does not feel like that. It feels permanent. It feels endless. It feels like you will never breathe again. But that is the lie emotion tells when it is un-examined.

I have been through the worst of the worst. I have witnessed tragedies directly in front of me. And because I did not yet have emotional awareness, I suffered longer and harder than I needed to. Not because my pain wasn't real, but because I did not know how to hold it. I did not believe I could experience healing and relief from my past.

Many horrible things have happened to so many people throughout their lives. A huge amount of us have endured trauma, abuse, death and disappointment. Some incidents have been so horrendous we do not feel we can ever move forward.

✦✦ When I was seventeen years old, less than thirty days away from my high school graduation, I personally witnessed a tragedy that changed my life forever.

My grandfather, grandmother, her youngest son who was my father, my sister and I lived in a large home in Compton. It had three gigantic bedrooms, a full size kitchen and service porch. There was a large separate living room and dining room, a long hallway, two bathrooms, and a massive backyard with a huge avocado tree. The property had another smaller home in the back that my father's sister SaBra (who I was named after) lived.

We were happy, healthy children, very well taken care of by

our grandmother.

My grandparents were both born in Dallas, Texas and were poor growing up as children, so they were determined to make sure they never experienced lack once they moved to California. We always had more than enough food. There was a large, deep freezer in our home that they kept stocked with food.

Quite often my grandmother would tell us stories of her childhood in Texas. She would tell us that she could take a quarter and buy and loaf of bread and a slab of salami. She told us so many stories of having only one pair of shoes and having to walk from North Dallas to South Dallas to school everyday. Looking back, I wish I would have paid more attention to those priceless stories.

My grandfather and grandmother did not have any children together. They met in Dallas after my grandmothers divorce from her first husband Charlie Fisher.

My sister and I were the only two children of her youngest son, so when our mother couldn't take care of us due to her drug addiction, my grandmother gladly took over. My sister and I were infants, only 11 and 3 months old when she took us into her home. She was sixty-nine years old and had already raised three children of her own. I'm sure the decision to take on children that most likely were born with drugs in their systems could not have been an easy one, but she did it wholeheartedly and willingly.

My grandfather was not the biological father of my grandmother's three children. He was her second husband who had moved her and her children to California from Dallas to give them a better life.

My grandmother didn't speak a lot about their relationship when we were children, but it was always clear to us even as small kids that he was not the love of her life. He was simply a nice man who was a great provider who moved her and her children from Dallas to California in the 1950's. I never knew my grandmother to work her husband was the sole provider in our household.

Although our grandfather lived in the home with us for the entire seventeen years my sister and I were there, I don't remember having a lot of personal interaction with him. I have no memory of any parental advice at all. I can clearly remember my father and my grandmother taking time to talk to and teach us things as we grew up but I don't ever remember my grandfather talking to us or telling us stories. In retrospect I find that unusual but it was just normal to us back then. I also don't recall having a need or urge to bond with him either.

He cut grass for a living so there were always large lawn mowers in our home. The only outfit I ever remember him wearing was a pair of green overalls. His legal name was McClendon Fair but we all called him Mack. He was a tall man, at least 6 foot 3 inches. I can't say for sure if he was soft spoken, I can only say that I don't have any real memory of what his voice sounded like. He spoke to us so rarely. He definitely never yelled at us or my grandmother. I don't even remember ever hearing them argue.

My last year of high school, I was alone in my room when my grandmother came into my room with a concerned look on her face. I was laying on my bed and she stood there with her hands on her hips with a worried look. She said, *"Mack said he was gonna kill me."* She seemed worried but, like I said I had never witnessed him abuse or even raise his voice at her our entire childhood.

Being raised in the church, I was taught that prayer fixes

everything. I responded and said to her *"Well Mama, if you know where he keeps the gun then please go take it and remove the bullets."* Once she left my room I got onto my knees and prayed, *"God, Mama doesn't seem happy. I love her, please make her happy."*

The next day was Sunday, May 3, 1997. I was only 17 years old but I was in a committed relationship with a young man who would later become my first husband. He worked as a security guard and was coming to pick me up one day after his shift. I was aimlessly walking through the house from room to room to pass the time until he arrived.

I went into my grandparents room which was a very large bedroom that had been added onto the home. It was the size of a large living room. I walked into their room and immediately noticed a gun laying on the television stand. I instantly reflected back to the conversation my grandmother and I had the day before when I had told her to remove the bullets from the gun. I walked over to the gun and picked it up. Only because of my boyfriend's profession and the fact that he carried a 357 magnum himself which he had recently demonstrated the workings of did I know how check the gun to see if my grandmother had indeed removed the bullets like I suggested to her the day before.

I picked up the gun, opened the cylinder, noticed that the bullets were still in the gun. I slowly started to turn the gun downward and allow the six bullets to slide out of the cylinder and into the palm of my hand. Instantly I thought, *"SaBrina you are being silly, they have been married for thirty-two years"* So I stopped just as the bullets were half way out and i turned the gun upward and let the bullets slide back into the gun. The gun was so old and rusty I was afraid to pop the cylinder closed.

My grandmother and grandfather were both in the kitchen. I

walked onto the service porch, which is next to the kitchen, and said to my grandfather as I held the gun with the open cylinder in my left hand. I said *"I opened your gun, but I'm afraid to close it."* He was sitting in his normal seat at the kitchen table and my grandmother was standing directly across from him. He looked up at me and responded, *"What are you doing with my gun? Do not play with guns!"* I replied, *"Clyde taught me how to open it."* Clyde was my current boyfriend.

My grandfather got up from the table and took the gun out of my hand and sat back down at the table. He sat the gun on the kitchen table and continued to lecture me about gun safety.

Instantly, my grandmother who was still standing picked up the gun and immediately turned it away from both of us pointing in the direction of a window that was behind her. She began to refer to the weight of the gun, she bounced it up and down saying *"This gun is heavy, Verie (who was a relative of hers) has a gun like this."* As soon as her hand came down from the bouncing, the gun went off behind her under the window. The startling sound caused me to run, but I heard my grandfather say to her, *"You tried to kill me."* I could hear his kitchen chair scraping the floor as he pushed back. I stopped and immediately returned to the doorway of the kitchen in time to see my grandfather remove the gun from my grandmother's hand and shoot her in the head.

Things appeared to be moving in slow motion. It seemed as though I saw the hole begin to form in my grandmothers head. I saw her body slowly begin to slump and fall to the ground. I believed I would be next, so I turned and ran through the house and out the front door. I kept running until I got six doors down to a neighbor's home. This was the house of childhood friends we had grown up with, Reuben, Lavonne and Craig (who would later become KAM, the famous rapper from Compton).

I ran up to the door and began to beat on the door hysterically. Someone opened the door and I began to scream, *"My grandfather killed my grandmother!"*

I'm not sure if I blacked out after that, but when I returned outside from their house the streets were blocked and there were loud sirens, it seemed like utter chaos. My entire world changed that day. Life as I knew it would never be the same.

I have carried the memory of that tragic day with me for years. I have replayed that memory over and over in my head for what felt like a lifetime. I re-traumatized myself with the visual images of my grandmothers lifeless body falling to the floor after being shot in the head by my grandfather, her husband of 32 years.

Although this happened when I was a child, I held this horrible memory in my mind for years and I suffered from it well into my late 40s. I had nightmares of that day for decades. The scene of her death played like a movie in my mind repeatedly. I had come to terms with the fact that I would forever be plagued with this memory and the pain of this devastating day. ✦✦

Had I known earlier that darkness does not cancel light, I would have been gentler with myself. If I would have known that emotions rise and fall like waves, I would not have feared them so deeply that I would be broken forever. I never thought I could ever heal from witnessing something so horrible, but healing is possible. Had I known that each new day carries even the smallest amount of relief, I would have clung to that instead of drowning in the moment.

That is why emotional awareness and Balance matters so much. There are people who have taken their own lives who did not want to die. They wanted the pain to stop. If someone had taught them that emotions are temporary visitors and not permanent residents, they might still be here. If someone had taught them how to pause, breathe, and ride the wave instead of becoming the wave, they might have survived that moment.

This is why emotional awareness should be taught early in life. It is not optional. It is essential. It is spiritual work of the highest order.

I am fifty-six years old now. I have raised four children. I ran a business for thirty years and employed over seventeen hundred women. I have lived through the worst. I have suffered from depression and PTSD. I have lost a maternal figure in my life who loved me. I have somehow managed to built while still being broken. I am committed, more than ever, to peace for the rest of my life. I want you to know that your pain can and will heal. you can fell better and lead a happy healthy life.

I am done screaming and hollering. I am done panicking out of fear. I am done living in in my past and reliving painful memories. Panic and pain no longer rule me, but working through it was a process.

After I started having children, the panic intensified. I would imagine danger everywhere. We could be at an amusement park, and I would glance at a roller coaster and my body would react as if one of my children had just fallen off of it. My heart would race. My stomach would drop and my chest would tighten. All of this from a thought. That is how powerful our thoughts are.

I would hear an ice cream truck. One of my kids would say, "Mommy, can I get ice cream?" and internally, my body would respond as if they had run into the street and been hit by the ice cream truck. Completely unfounded. Totally imagined. Completely overwhelming.

At the time, I did not know what was happening to me. I thought I was just anxious. I thought I was just an overprotective mother. What I did not understand was that I was living with post-traumatic stress.

Back then, especially in Black families, you did not talk about trauma. Families did not go to therapy. They did not unpack emotions. You sucked it up and kept moving. Pain was something you survived quietly. There were no tools or therapy. No talking about it and no emotional support.

But trauma does not disappear because you ignore it. It waits on you. It shows up later in your body or in your reactions. In panic attacks or fear you can't explain. Emotional awareness helped me name that. Learning the art of *Balance* helped me heal it.

Healing did not happen overnight. It something I had to seek out. It was a long process that i had to commit to. Healing happened when I stopped shaming myself for my reactions and started understanding them. It happened when I learned to pause instead of panic. When I learned to observe instead of explode. I mad a conscious choice to stop the impulsive behavior and realize, most of the world does not know what I have been through. Many have there own traumas to heal from.

When I learned to take control of my own story and accept that I can not go back and change that terrible day, but I do not have to relive it for the rest of my life. Nor does it define who I am today.

Spiritual work is learning how to stay present with yourself even when it is uncomfortable. It is allowing yourself to feel without losing control. It is learning how to think first, and then respond instead of react.

I am ready now to live the most peaceful life I have ever known.

I am ready to enjoy the beauty of the land of enchantment, New Mexico. The Sandia Mountains. The beautiful pink and purple skies. The stillness and reverence for the ancient architecture. I am ready to live the second half of my life in a calm peaceful space.

That peace did not come from avoiding pain. It came from learning how to be emotionally aware. It came from remembering that I am a spiritual being and the worst battles happen inside our mind. Finding **Balance** changed my life for the better and it will do the same for you.

If you are reading this and you see yourself in my story, I want you to know this. You are not broken. You are not weak. You are not failing at spirituality because you still feel deeply. Emotional awareness is not about eliminating emotion. It is about understanding it.

This work continues for as long as we are alive, and that is not a burden, it is a gift. Every day you choose awareness, you choose peace. Every day you pause first, you protect your future. Every day you breathe instead of explode, you honor your spirit.

Emotional awareness is spiritual work, it is the work of waking up to who you truly are.

5

Finding Balance Through Peace

There was a time in my life when I believed that being busy meant being successful. My days were full, my weeks were packed, and my life was complicated in ways I didn't even question. I ran my business seven days a week. Not five. Not six, but Seven long days a week. I did that for twenty-six years, it never once occurred to me that I should take a day off. I seemed to forget hat I was the boss and that I made the rules, so I could change them.

Rest was not part of my vocabulary. Slowing down felt irresponsible. I wore exhaustion like a badge of honor because I thought that was what strength looked like. I was making a lot of money but too tired to spend it.

Everything changed after I turned fifty. A health scare has a way of interrupting the stories we tell ourselves. It stops the noise and It cuts through denial. When the doctor told me I had a tumor in my head, one that had already taken eighty percent of the hearing in my left ear, I felt something shift instantly. Not panic or hysteria. Just a deep, quiet knowing that said, *You cannot live the same way anymore.*

The tumor had a name. Glomus tympanicum. a very rare, slow growing tumor. But a serious one. It had already eaten away the incus and the malus ear bones. Surgery would eventually be necessary, but not immediately. What I didn't know then was that it would take five years before UCLA Medical Center could finally perform that surgery. Five years of living with something inside my head that could not be ignored. Somehow it was connected to the same blood supply as my heart, so when my heart beat so did the tumor. Reminding me daily that there was in invader in my body.

I understood something very clearly during that season. If I was going to walk around with a tumor in my head, I could not afford to be stressed. Not emotionally or mentally. Stress was no longer an inconvenience. It was a threat to my quality of my life.

At the time, I still had four employees at Braids by SaBrina. One of them, in particular, was draining me. She was a functional drug addict. She was always late to work and always rude to customers. She was constantly bringing chaos into a space that required peace and professionalism. I had tolerated it for far too long, telling myself stories about loyalty, patience, and compassion while ignoring what my body was telling me.

This time, I listened. I sat down and I prayed. Not one of those rushed prayers. A real detailed one. The kind where you sit quietly long enough to hear the answer. And the answer was immediate and unmistakable. *This cannot continue.*

I knew that maintaining peace was no longer optional. It was essential to my well being. I also knew that peace does not coexist with constant disruption. So I made one of the hardest, yet healthiest decisions of my life. I wished those employees well and sent them on their way. I terminated all four of them that day.

During my prayer God had given me a new vision that involved creating a scared space of peace and wellness. I got up and the next day changed the name of the salon from Braids By SaBrina to A New Vision Dreadlock Studio. I called the sign people and created new signs, banners and business cards. It was a New day and I now had a New Vision. I had a vision that involved peace and tranquility for my life.

From that moment on, I lived stress-free intentionally. I worked alone in my salon, one client at a time. No more staff meant no more open door policy. I locked my door, raised my prices and greeted one client a day. Somehow I made more money that I had ever made in the history of the salon.

People misunderstand the phrase stress free because they assume it means a life where nothing difficult ever happens. That interpretation sets people up for disappointment, because no human life is free of challenges, unexpected events, or moments that test your strength. Stress free does not mean problem free. It means choice filled. It means you become conscious about what you are allowing into your life and what you are no longer willing to carry. You decide what deserves your energy and what no longer does. Over time you begin to understand that constant chaos is not something you have to tolerate simply because it has always been there. You become far more selective about what situations you step into and which ones you quietly step away from. Access to your time, your peace, and your attention is no longer given freely to everyone and everything that asks for it. The habit of entertaining unnecessary stress begins to fall away because you start recognizing that much of the pressure people live under is not inevitable. It is often the result of patterns that were never questioned. Choosing a simpler life becomes an intentional act rather than something that just happens by accident.

For years, I did exactly that. I simplified my schedule and my responsibilities. I scrubbed my environment of drama and chaos. I no longer had the stress of staff so I serviced one deadlock client at a time and no longer accepted walk ins which allowed me to keep my front door closed unless I was expecting a client. The physical environment around me changed dramatically because I was no longer allowing the constant unpredictability that used to define my days. There was no steady stream of people walking in with demands and emergencies. There was no pressure to manage a team of employees while also trying to manage my own health and emotions. Each appointment became something I could prepare for and fully focus on without feeling pulled in ten different directions. I created a completely stress free environment. I simplified my life because my life depended on it.

Those five years taught me more about peace than anything else ever could have. Peace is not passive. Peace is active, it is a choice. Maintaining peace requires effort and clarity about what belongs in your life and what does not. Boundaries become necessary because peace cannot exist where everything and everyone is allowed unlimited access to you. Letting go is often part of that process, even when it is painful. Some relationships, habits, or environments no longer fit the version of yourself that is trying to survive and heal. I had to distance myself from a few family member as well. That decision was not made out of anger or rejection. It came from the understanding that protecting your health and your peace sometimes means stepping back from dynamics that keep pulling you back into stress and emotional exhaustion.

Even with all of that intention, fear still showed up sometimes. I want to be honest about that. Positivity does not cancel humanity. Creating a peaceful life does not suddenly erase every emotional reaction that comes with facing something serious or uncertain. I made the mistake of joining a Facebook group for people with Glomus tumors. Big mistake that was. Every day I saw pictures of people with the side of their head shaved revealing their surgical scars. The images were raw reminders of the physical reality of what other people had gone through. Even with all the inner work I had done, even with all the spiritual tools I had practiced, there were moments where I was afraid. Those moments did not mean the peace I had built was fake or fragile. They simply meant I was still human, still processing something difficult, and still learning how to hold both courage and vulnerability at the same time.

Five years later on January 2nd, 3rd, and 4th of 2025. Three days that changed everything. The glomus tympanicum tumor was removed by Dr. Akira Ishiyama at UCLA Medical Center. The incus and malus bones that had been eaten away were replaced with titanium. The surgery was successful. But before the surgery, I had fear. there were many possible complications they came in to tell me about right before surgery.

I had trained myself to be positive, yes. I had trained myself to regulate my emotions, yes. But I am human, so I am not immune to fear. Sitting with the reality of brain-adjacent surgery does something to you. Especially when you have been warned of potential outcomes. One of the possibilities the doctors prepared me for was facial paralysis.

That fear was real. The morning of the surgery, I put on my headset. I listened to my sound bowls. I breathed deeply and intentionally. I slowed my heart rate to stay calm. I reminded my body that it was safe even when my mind was scared. I did not shame myself for feeling fear. I soothed myself through it.

The surgery was successful. My face was not paralyzed. I was spared in ways I do not take lightly. I am deeply aware of how blessed I am. During that journey, I encountered two other people who had the same rare tumor. They were not as fortunate. Both experienced facial paralysis after their surgeries.

It is part of why I am so committed to living this way forever. That chapter of my life taught me something sacred. Peace is not something you return to after the storm. It is something you build before the storm arrives.

Simplifying my life saved me from panic and hysteria. It taught me how to listen to my body. How to honor my nervous system and protect my energy. How to let go without guilt and choose myself without apologizing for it. Those rituals I developed during that time are not temporary. They are permanent. I am keeping them for the rest of my life, and I am teaching them to my children.

Because even the most positive person will experience stress. Even the most spiritually grounded person will feel fear. Balance is not about never being shaken. It is about knowing how to calm yourself when you are.

Simplifying life does not mean shrinking it. It means removing what drains you so what nourishes you can breathe. It means asking hard questions about what you tolerate and why. It means recognizing when loyalty to old patterns is costing you your health.

Peace does not come from adding more. It comes from subtracting what no longer serves you. I am living proof that simplification is not weakness. It is wisdom earned. It is strength refined and alignment chosen again and again.

I survived that season. I healed. I am here, happy and committed to living in a way that honors that miracle every single day.

If there is one thing I want you to take from this chapter, it is this. You do not have to wait for a crisis to simplify your life. You do not have to wait for your body to force the lesson. You can choose peace now. Gently and intentionally.

Simplify your life, reclaim peace, and protect it like your life depends on it. Because sometimes, it truly does.

6

Loving Me Again

Before there was fear, there was love. Before there was pain, there was love. Before there were rules, expectations, labels, and stories about who you had to be, there was love.

That is our true nature. We are pure love made in the image of God. For some, that idea feels natural and comforting. For others, it may feel distant or even unrealistic in a world that so often appears harsh and unforgiving. We wake up each morning to headlines filled with chaos, tragedy, and division. We scroll through images of suffering and injustice before our feet even touch the floor. It can begin to feel as though love is fragile, rare, or reserved only for certain moments or certain people.

Yet, I believe this with my whole heart. Beneath everything we see, beneath everything we have been taught to fear, mankind's true nature is love. We are all pure love. Anytime we are experiencing emotions that are opposite of love, or exhibiting behaviors that are not motivated by love, we are operating outside of our true God given nature. That does not make us bad. It makes us disconnected and imbalanced.

We are not born angry, bitter, guarded, or emotionally closed off from the world around us. Those qualities are not present in a newborn child. Human beings enter life with openness, curiosity, and a natural desire to connect. When you look at a baby, you are looking at a human being who has not yet learned fear of rejection, shame about who they are, or the belief that they must earn the right to be loved. A child does not arrive questioning whether they deserve affection, kindness, or belonging. The instinctive nature of a child is to reach outward, to explore, to trust, and to respond to love with love. There is something deeply expansive about that early state of being, something pure that exists before the world begins to shape our beliefs about ourselves. That original nature reflects a sense of wholeness that does not need to be earned or proven. Worthiness exists from the very beginning of life.

Many belief systems have taught generations of people that they entered the world already flawed, already broken, already carrying some kind of spiritual debt that must be repaid in order to be accepted by God or by society. That idea has been repeated so often that many people accept it without ever questioning where it came from or whether it truly reflects the nature of human life. The message that a person must prove their value before they are worthy of love or grace has shaped how countless individuals see themselves. Yet when you observe a newborn child, nothing about that life suggests something damaged or morally corrupt. What you see instead is innocence, openness, and a complete lack of the self judgment that adults often carry. The idea that we arrived here fundamentally flawed contradicts the reality of how human life actually begins. At birth there is no bitterness, no resentment, and no self hatred. Those things develop later through experiences, conditioning, and the beliefs we absorb from the world around us.

Life slowly begins to shape our understanding of ourselves, and that shaping often begins earlier than we realize. Childhood becomes the stage where many of the first messages about worthiness are delivered, sometimes intentionally and sometimes without anyone meaning to cause harm. Words spoken by authority figures, criticism that lingers longer than encouragement, and moments of rejection or comparison can begin planting quiet doubts in a child's mind. Over time those doubts grow into internal narratives that follow a person well into adulthood. A child who once felt naturally confident and secure may slowly begin questioning whether they are good enough, smart enough, attractive enough, or deserving enough. Instead of growing into life with the belief that love and belonging are their birthright, many people begin believing they must constantly prove themselves in order to receive the acceptance they once felt naturally.

That shift creates a lifelong pattern that many individuals never fully recognize. The pursuit of validation begins to replace the quiet confidence that once existed naturally. People spend years striving to earn approval, affection, and recognition that they believe must be achieved through performance, success, or sacrifice. What began as a simple desire for connection slowly becomes a relentless search for confirmation that they are worthy. Relationships, careers, achievements, and social recognition often become the arenas where this search plays out. Underneath those pursuits there is often a deeper longing to reclaim a sense of self worth that was never meant to be lost in the first place.

Every person carries a different story about how that sense of worthiness became buried. Some people experienced harsh criticism growing up. Others faced rejection, betrayal, or environments where love felt conditional. Some learned early that mistakes brought shame instead of understanding. Others absorbed cultural messages that defined value through appearance, wealth, status, or perfection. Regardless of the specific story, the emotional outcome often looks similar. Men, women, and children all carry their own versions of the same quiet question about whether they are truly enough as they are.

In a healthier world, children would grow up with their natural sense of value protected and reinforced rather than gradually eroded. Young people would be taught that their worth is not dependent on perfection, performance, or comparison with others. Confidence would develop from knowing that mistakes are part of growth rather than evidence of failure. A child raised with that understanding would step into adulthood with a much stronger foundation, capable of taking responsibility for their life without constantly questioning their right to exist, to succeed, or to be loved. That kind of upbringing would allow people to grow into their full potential without spending decades trying to repair a self image that was damaged long before they understood what was happening.

The difficulty, however, is that life rarely unfolds in a controlled or predictable way. Experiences arrive without asking whether we feel prepared to handle them. Challenges do not wait until a person feels emotionally strong enough to navigate them. Difficult moments appear suddenly and sometimes repeatedly, creating situations that test our sense of stability and identity. There are seasons when life feels expansive and full of possibility, moments when everything seems to align and joy feels natural. There are also seasons when events feel overwhelming, confusing, and painful in ways that shake our confidence in ourselves and in the world around us.

Learning to live through both kinds of seasons becomes one of the most important challenges of being human. The goal is not to avoid hardship entirely because that is impossible. What matters is developing the inner strength to move through those experiences without allowing them to convince us that we are broken or unworthy. Hard moments can either deepen our understanding of ourselves or slowly push us toward bitterness and self destruction if we lose sight of our inherent value. Navigating life requires remembering something that many people forget along the way. The hardships we encounter may shape our journey, but they do not define our worth as human beings.

The trauma we have been through does not change who you are. It changes how you survive it. For a long time, I did not understand that distinction. I judged my younger self harshly and without mercy. I questioned why I had such a temper in my twenties. Why I was explosive. Why my reactions were so intense. Why was I mad at God. Why my voice got loud before my heart could explain itself. I assumed something was wrong with me because my own mother was incapable of raising me. I believed I was broken and unworthy. I told myself I had failed spiritually, emotionally, and as a woman trying to evolve. I had a lot of internal pain and no where to put it.

But I was wrong. Nothing was wrong with me. I was responding to pain I did not yet know how to hold. I either suppressed it our let it out viciously. The trauma I experienced did not reflect my true nature. It pulled me away from myself. Not because I was weak, but because I was human. When you experience trauma, your body learns to brace itself for more. When you witness violence, your nervous system learns vigilance. When you lose safety early in life, survival becomes the priority long before peace ever has a chance to settle in.

I am not blaming myself anymore, I am understanding myself. There is a difference. I am not still angry with anyone from my past. I forgive them all energetically and spiritually, and that for my own peace.

Understanding the root of your behavior is not an excuse to continue it. But it causes you to have more compassion for yourself. It is the doorway back to who you truly are. **Without** understanding, we punish ourselves for our coping mechanisms. **With** understanding, we begin to gently loosen our grip on them. We show ourselves love.

I know now that the anger was grief that had nowhere to go. The fear was love trying to protect what had already been hurt. The hardness was softness that never felt safe enough to rest. That realization changed everything for me.

When we judge ourselves endlessly, we stay trapped in who we once were. When we take the time understand ourselves, we create space to return to who we are, and who we are, beneath every layer of defense, beneath every story we tell ourselves, is love.

Love is not something you earn. Love is your birthright, it is something you deserve, before, during and after healing. Love is not something you receive only once you are perfect. Love is what you are.

Returning to yourself is not about becoming someone new. It is about remembering who you were before the world taught you to armor up. It is about slowly peeling back the layers of survival so that your true nature can breathe again.

This is where stillness becomes essential. Learning to be quiet and still long enough to gain control over the mental images you focus on will prove to be one of the most valuable tools in your personal growth. The mind is powerful, but it is also impressionable. What you allow it to focus on will eventually shape how you feel, how you react, and how you see yourself.

Even if at first you can only find ten minutes a day to steal away, take those ten minutes. Sit somewhere quiet. Close your eyes. Breathe deeply and intentionally. Notice where your thoughts go without judging them. Over time, you will find creative ways to take more moments for yourself. These small pauses begin to add up. They become anchors throughout your day.

As this becomes a routine practice in your life, you will begin to see its value. You will notice how quickly your body responds to gentleness. You will recognize how much of your tension was learned, not inherent. You will start to feel the difference between reacting and responding.

Returning to a place of love always starts internally. Learning to love myself after years of doing the opposite was not automatic. It was a conscious decision. No one approached me daily to remind me that I was unwanted or unworthy. I told myself that. I replayed old narratives. I repeated conclusions that were formed in moments of pain, not truth.

Eventually, I had to face a difficult realization. I was the one continuing the damage. And that also meant I was the only one who could reverse it. I had to make the choice to initiate my own healing. That realization was not heavy. It was empowering.

Because if I had the power to wound myself with my thoughts, then I also had the power to heal myself with them. Returning to yourself does not require perfection. It requires honesty. It requires patience and your willingness to sit with yourself long enough to hear what you actually need.

This chapter is not about fixing yourself. It is about coming home. It is about remembering that beneath every reaction, every defense, every scar, there is still a part of you that knows how to love and be loved. That part has never left. It has only been waiting.

Returning to yourself is the final act of balance. It is where emotional balance, spiritual balance, and self compassion meet. It is the moment you stop searching outward and begin listening inward. It is the quiet understanding that nothing was ever missing. You were always here. And you were always perfect.

We forget that because life teaches us to judge ourselves and others. it teaches us to compare and label. To condemn and judge ourselves for our mistakes. We judge others for theirs. We judge people for where they are instead of honoring who they are becoming.

Judgment is separation from our true nature. Love is remembrance and re-connection.

When you stop judging yourself, you soften and become kinder. When you stop judging others, you open your heart and mind and when enough people do that inner work, something extraordinary becomes possible for the world.

Collective healing begins with individual responsibility. Mankind can not evolve as a whole until we all evolve individually. We do not heal the world by pointing fingers. We heal the world by returning to ourselves and returning to love. We help to heal the world by doing the quiet, unseen work of self-awareness. By choosing peace when chaos would be easier. By choosing love when fear feels justified.

Each person who commits to balance, to awareness, to love, contributes to the evolution of humanity. This is not spiritual fantasy. This is energetic truth. That is how we create a world that we want our grandchildren to live in.

People often say they don't want to bring children into this world because the world feels so dark. I understand that fear. But I also know this. There is still so much beauty here. There is still hope here. This world can be a magical place. We choose how we perceive it.

We get to design our lives. We get to choose how we respond. We get to choose what we nurture. We choose what we pass down to the generation that come behind us.

This earth is still a miracle. Being alive is still a blessing, and you still have more power than you've been taught to believe. I feel this deeply in my fifties. More deeply than I ever have before. At fifty-six years old, I am returning to myself. Not reinventing or becoming someone new. Returning to my true self. I am peeling away layers and letting go of armor. I am finally releasing survival patterns that once saved me but are no longer needed.

I am returning to the woman God intended me to be. The person before the trauma and fear. I am returning to woman before the anger and sadness.

That woman is perfect and gentle. She is joyful, happy and grounded. That woman is wise and loving. She is strong without being hard. She is soft without being fragile.

The abandonment I experienced as a child was not my fault. Witnessing my grandmother's life taken in front of me was not my fault. The survival strategies I developed were not failures. They were responses, and now, with awareness, I get to choose differently. There is beauty in being able to make a different choice.

That is what returning to yourself looks like. It is not erasing the past. It is integrating it with the new found you. Honoring what you survived while no longer letting it define how you live.

I want this for every person reading these words. I want you to know that no matter what you have been through, your true nature is still intact. It may be buried. It may be guarded. It may feel distant. But it is there, within you. Life did not destroy it.

Your true nature is waiting, waiting for you to come home. You are not too damaged to return to yourself. You are not too late, it is never too late. You are not beyond repair.

There is nothing you have done and nothing that has been done to you that disqualifies you from divine love. It all begins with you, with self.

Self-love is not narcissism. You are not cocky or self-absorbed when you focus on yourself first. Self-love is restoration. It is remembering your worth without needing permission. It is building an authentic self-esteem that is not dependent on approval, performance, or perfection.

When you love yourself deeply, you stop chasing validation. When you love yourself deeply, you stop abandoning yourself. When you love yourself deeply, you stop tolerating harm, and when enough people do that, relationships change. Families change and communities change. The world changes.

All things are possible in this amazing world we live in. I know that not as a slogan, but it is how I live. Statistically, I should not be alive. Based on statistics my life should have ended in tragedy. Statistically, the woman I am today should not exist. Yet, here I am.

Alive and breathing, healing, writing this book. Loving on myself and teaching others to do the same. I am still here creating life changing content. Offering my life not as proof of perfection, but as proof of possibility.

What you once considered the mess of your life can become your message that changes the life of another. The things you survived are not meant to shame you. They are meant to shape your wisdom and solidify your growth. The pain you carry is not a life sentence. It is raw material for transformation. And transformation is possible for us all.

One day, the very thing you thought broke you will be the thing that helps someone else survive. That is alchemy and amazing grace. That is love in action.

Returning to yourself is returning to love. Not the romanticized version that ignores pain or bypasses truth, but the real kind of love. The kind that tells the truth without cruelty and forgives without forgetting the lesson. The love that stays present even when things feel uncomfortable. This is the love that does not abandon you in moments of fear or failure. This is the love that does not demand perfection before offering acceptance. This is the kind of love that waits patiently for you to come back home to yourself.

Returning to love does not mean pretending that pain never happened. It means choosing peace without denying what hurt you. It means choosing hope without ignoring reality. It means choosing love without conditions, even when the past tries to convince you that love must be earned or proven. True balance does not come from avoiding hardship. It comes from learning how to meet life with honesty, compassion, and **Balance**

When we talk about emotional balance, we are not talking about a life without challenges. We are talking about a life where challenges no longer define your worth. Emotional balance begins the moment you stop fighting yourself and start listening. It begins when you recognize that your reactions are messengers, not enemies. It begins when you allow yourself to slow down long enough to hear what your heart has been asking for all along.

"Be still and know that I am God." These words are not

an invitation to escape the world. They are an invitation to remember who you are within it. Stillness is not weakness, it is strength that has learned to trust. In a world that constantly demands your attention, your productivity, and your performance, choosing stillness is an act of courage. It is in stillness that the noise quiets enough for truth to rise.

No matter how busy our daily lives become, taking intentional time to sit and reflect can remove unnecessary stress from our day. Stillness allows the nervous system to settle. It allows the mind to soften its grip on fear. It reminds us that we are not machines designed only to produce and perform. We are valuable, creative beings made in the image of God, capable of growth, healing, and transformation. When we slow down, we remember that we are not powerless passengers in our lives. We are active participants in shaping how we respond to the world around us.

Returning to love means returning to your true nature. Before the trauma. Before the conditioning. Before the stories you were told about who you had to be in order to be accepted. It means taking responsibility for the thoughts you allow to live rent free in your mind. Especially the ones connected to past pain. The events themselves have passed, but when we replay them repeatedly without awareness, we unknowingly reopen wounds that are asking to heal. We relive moments that no longer exist and call it protection, when in reality it is self harm disguised as memory.

Emotional balance requires discernment. It asks you to notice when reflection turns into rumination. It invites you to gently interrupt patterns that keep you anchored to a version of yourself that survived but never fully lived. Healing does not require forgetting what happened to you. It requires choosing not to let the past dictate the present. You are allowed to remember without reliving it all. You are allowed to honor what you endured without remaining imprisoned by it.

Returning to yourself means going within without judgment. It means sitting with yourself long enough to recognize your own voice again. This is the voice that knows when something is misaligned. This is the voice that guides you back toward peace when you have wandered too far from yourself.

Go within and sit with yourself without rushing to fix anything. Listen gently to what comes up. Be patient with the parts of you that learned to protect instead of trust. Be kind to the version of you that did the best it could with the awareness it had at the time.

Authentic self love is not loud. It does not demand attention or validation. It is quiet and steady. It is the way you speak to yourself when no one else is listening. It is the boundaries you honor even when they are inconvenient. It is the compassion you extend to yourself when you fall short of expectations that were never yours to begin with. Self love is not indulgence. It is integrity. It is alignment between what you believe, what you feel, and how you live.

Balance is not found in perfection or constant positivity. It is found in presence and in your willingness to stay connected to yourself even when emotions rise and fall. Mind, body, and energy are not separate systems competing for control. They are parts of a whole that communicate with each other continuously. When one is ignored, the others respond. When one is honored, the others begin to align.

If you ever doubt that transformation is possible, let my life be your reminder. I am here because I chose to listen instead of run. I am here because I chose understanding over self punishment.

BALANCE

I am still here because I chose to return to myself even when it felt unfamiliar and uncomfortable. I survived not because I was unbreakable, but because I was willing to come back to love again and again. You can do the same.

This book was never meant to give you all the answers. It was meant to help you remember where to look. The work does not end here. The journey does not stop with the last page. This is not the end of your healing. It is the beginning of a deeper relationship with yourself. A relationship built on honesty, patience, and love.

Every time you pause before reacting, you are choosing balance. Each time you soften instead of hardening, you are choosing alignment. When you return to yourself instead of abandoning yourself, you are choosing love. Emotional balance does not require a perfect life. It requires a present one.

Carry this with you as you move forward. You are perfect and unbroken. You are becoming the best version of yourself daily. You are not lost. You are learning how to come home. You are not separate from love. You are made of it.

This is not the end.

This is the beginning. I love You

7

Being Balanced Emotionally

If you met me in business, you might think you knew exactly who I was. I was confident, decisive, authoritative, focused. Plus I was kinda cute too. I was the woman who runs the room, sets the tone, makes the call, and moves things forward without hesitation. All by myself because I didn't not need anyone elses help. I was the woman who handled responsibility like second nature and did not fold under pressure. The woman who figured it out because there is no other option. That version of me is real, she still exist to this day. She is strong, resilient and reliable. She is the reason my family survived, my children thrived, and my businesses existed consistently for thirty years.

But that version of me is not the whole story. Inside, I am also soft and tender. I am emotional. I cry easily and I feel very deeply. I am emotionally moved by beauty, by music, by love and close connections. I love meaningful conversations. I am the woman who gets misty over memories and overwhelmed by gratitude. I am the one who believes she can change the world. The one who loves softness, warmth, affection, and expression. I am the one who loves pink and has a entire soft pick home office. I love dressing up in pretty dresses, makeup, with my hair done just right. I am feminine in ways that have nothing to do with weakness and everything to do with feeling alive.

For a long time, I thought these two parts of me were in conflict. I thought I had to choose which one I wanted to be. I thought strength meant suppressing softness and softness meant letting go of strength. Life taught me otherwise.

When you are responsible for four children, when you are the one making sure bills are paid, food is on the table, and stability exists, softness becomes a luxury you do not always have access to. There are moments in life where you simply do what needs to be done. You do not hesitate, and you can not crumble. You do not have time to wait for permission from others. You get your butt up and rise. You learn to act quickly because you have to protect and provide. That kind of strength is not optional, it's instinctual. It is God given maternal instinct. It is primal. It is love in action.

During those seasons, it is almost impossible to be soft. Not because softness disappears, but because strength has to take the lead. When survival is on the line, and responsibility is heavy, when others are depending on you, there is no room for fragility in the moment. There is only movement forward. I moved forward again and again and again, and I don't regret a minute. It trained me for the real world.

I built my businesses the same way. When I opened my braiding salon, Braids By SaBrina, when I launched my tattoo shop, Inked 4 Life Tattoo Studio, and when I started my publishing company, In59Seconds Publishing Co, I had to step fully into my masculine energy. Those seasons required planning, structure, vision, execution, and leadership. There was no space for indecision. No room for emotional wavering. I had to be clear. I had to be firm and grounded. I needed to be respected and heard. I had to be strong.

This is not to say that women are not capable of strength, leadership, or execution. I am a woman, and I lived it. What I am saying is that masculine energy does not mean becoming a man or wanting to be one. It means accessing the focused, decisive, action-oriented energy that already exists within all of us. Masculine and feminine energies are not about gender. They are about function.

We all carry both energies, and we move between them depending on what life requires of us. There are seasons that demand softness, intuition, and surrender, and there are seasons that demand direction, authority, and action. During those building years, I was exactly where I needed to be. I wasn't out of balance. I was in alignment.

What saved me, though, was learning early on that I could not live there permanently. I understood that masculine energy is powerful, but it is not meant to dominate every area of life. It is meant to support, not override. To build, not harden. To lead, not disconnect.

I am a feminine woman. That is not something I had to learn. It is something I had to allow. I love beauty, adornment and softness. I love being held, being seen and cherished by a man. I love creating from inspiration instead of pressure. I love relaxing into the flow instead of forcing. These things are not contradictions to my strength. They are the reason my strength does not destroy me.

One of the most important lessons I learned was understanding where each energy belongs. Business requires a certain level of masculine energy. Structure, authority, clarity, boundaries. Relationships require a different balance. You cannot come

BALANCE

home from work and bark orders at your partner like they are an employee. You cannot carry the same tone, posture and energy from the boardroom into your bedroom and expect intimacy to survive.

I learned that lesson early in life, and it saved me in ways I did not fully understand at the time. None of my relationships would have survived if I had not learned how to shift gears. Strength has to know when to soften. Authority has to know when to yield, and leadership must know when to listen.

That does not mean becoming smaller. It means becoming more intelligent with your energy. You are in control of the energy you put out.

There were times when I was better at balancing this in business than I was in other areas of my life. I knew how to compartmentalize professionally. But personally, it was harder. Old wounds, emotional exhaustion, and the pressure of responsibility sometimes blurred the lines. I would bring armor into places that needed openness. Many many times I brought control into moments that needed trust. I am honest enough with myself to admit that I am still learning. I am still a work in progress.

But I love both sides of me, and I want you all to love and embrace both sides of you. I love the woman in me who never gives up. The Leo alpha female who is passionate, determined, and unstoppable when it comes to protecting what matters. I love the woman who will get up no matter how tired she is and do what needs to be done. I also love the woman who can hold her ground, speak her truth, and stand tall in rooms that were not designed for her. I embrace the woman who feels safe enough to cry. The woman who feels the pain of others. The woman who wants softness, beauty, romance, and tenderness. The woman who enjoys being feminine without apology. I am aware that vulnerability is not weakness, it is courage in its most purest form.

When strength meets softness, something powerful happens. You stop living in extremes. You stop burning yourself out trying to prove something to someone else. You begin to live from integration and balance. True strength knows how to rest, and real softness knows how to stand firm. One without the other is incomplete. Every human being needs a perfect balance of both.

Many women are taught that they must harden themselves to survive, especially in leadership roles. Unfortunately many men are taught that they must suppress softness to be respected. Both teachings are lies. The most grounded people are those who can be firm without being cruel and gentle without being passive.

Softness does not cancel your authority, it humanizes it. Strength does not cancel femininity, it protects it. When you embrace both energies within you, you no longer feel divided inside. You stop feeling like you are switching masks depending on the room. You become consistent in your essence, even when your energy shifts to meet the moment.

There is a freedom that comes from loving all of yourself. From no longer apologizing for your ambition or your sensitivity. From no longer shrinking one part to make room for another. You realize that the softness is what keeps your strength from becoming bitter, and the strength is what keeps your softness from becoming fragile.

This is the balance I believe God intended for us all. I continue to practice maintaining balance because I truly believe life for everyone improves when balance is all areas of our lives is achieved. I am not saying it is easy to do. It is something we have to learn and consciously work at. But I believe it is worth the effort. Mental, spiritual, emotional balance, in my opinion is the key to a better life.

I no longer see my tears as a liability. I no longer see my leadership as a flaw. I do not see my femininity as something that needs to be hidden in order to be taken seriously. I allow myself to be layered, complex, and whole, and you should too.

Strength when it meets softness becomes wisdom. It becomes discernment and divine alignment. Alignment does not ask you to change who you are. It asks you to honor all of it. That is where real balance and happiness live.

8

Daily Practices to Help You Achieve Balance

If there is one thing life has taught me, it is this: balance does not happen by accident. It is not something you stumble into one day and keep forever. Balance is something you return to, over and over again, sometimes multiple times in a single day. And the way you return to it is through ritual and repetition.

When people hear the word ritual, they often think it has to be some secret routine and is against their old school religious beliefs. they think is complicated or spiritual in a formal way, or time-consuming. That could not be further from the truth. Ritual is simply anything you do intentionally to bring yourself back to center. It it routine and habitual behavior that you consciously choose. It is a choice create habit that improve your life or bring you joy and peace. It can be a simple pause, a planned moment of stillness and silence. A moment where you say, "I matter enough to regulate myself instead of reacting."

I have many daily rituals, and they did not all appear at once. They came from necessity. From stress and from moments where my body told me very clearly that I could not keep pushing without grounding myself first.

When I am in creation mode, especially, I can feel how easily stress creeps in. Creation is beautiful, but it is also demanding. There is excitement, momentum, and purpose in building something from the ground up, but there is also pressure. Pressure to get it right or to move faster. Pressure to keep up with the vision in your head. When I was setting up In59Seconds Publishing Company, I stepped into an entirely new world all at once. File formats. Conversion and uploads, daily downloads, extensive editing and learning digital platforms and systems. Things that, for years, my college-educated daughters handled effortlessly for me. Suddenly, I was the one who had to understand it all, and I had to understand it quickly.

I am a massive marketer by nature. I move with confidence when I believe in something. Once I announced the company, clients began lining up almost immediately. People wanted their books published. They trusted me. They were excited, and because of that, I felt an unspoken responsibility to perform at a high level right away. There was no easing into it. No gentle learning curve. I dove in headfirst, it is truly normal for me. I was working long hours, pushing myself mentally, emotionally, and physically because that is what I had always done when something mattered to me.

The truth is, I love working hard and building. I really enjoy creating a lot. But loving something does not mean it cannot consume you if you are not careful. This is a key area where so many people can benefit from learning balance. I had absolutely no work–life balance at that time. My days blended into nights and my mind never shut off. I dreamed about whatever idea I was working on. I know that energy very well. I call it "The Inspiration for Creation." Even when I sat down, my body was still in work mode. My nervous system never got the message that it was safe to rest. I still struggle with that at times.

Here is what no one really talks about. You can be doing something you love and still be harming yourself in the process. Passion does not cancel out exhaustion. Purpose does not protect you from burnout. Just because the work is meaningful does not mean your body is not keeping score. I learned the systems. I mastered them in record time. I am actually very proud of that. But I am also honest about the toll it took on me.

There were moments when I could feel my blood pressure spike without warning. Times when my chest felt tight and heavy. Many situations when my jaw clenched so hard I did not even realize I was holding tension until it started to ache. My breathing became shallow, and I truly don't believe in that. My body does not whisper when it is overwhelmed. It speaks loudly, and over the years, I have learned that ignoring those signals never leads anywhere good.

Work–life balance is not about laziness. It is not about doing less because you are incapable. It is about sustainability, and understanding that you cannot pour endlessly from a cup that never gets refilled. When you live in constant output mode, your body eventually forces a pause. It is always better to choose rest intentionally than to be forced into it through illness, anxiety, or emotional shutdown.

I had to learn how to step out of masculine, action-driven energy when the workday ended and consciously return to feminine energy. To soften and breathe. To just sit down and relax my body and my mind. I had to allow myself moments of stillness without feeling guilty. Balance does not mean you stop building. It means you learn when to step back so that building does not cost you your peace, your health, or your joy.

This is what true work–life balance looks like. Not perfectly divided hours, or rigid schedules. Becoming awareness and listening to our body is something beneficial that we must teach ourselves. Understanding that rest is not a reward for finishing everything, because the work will never truly be finished. Rest is a requirement for longevity, and when you learn that, you stop burning yourself out in the name of success and start building a life that can actually hold the success you are creating.

In those moments when I would stop. I would open YouTube and turn on binaural beats. Frequencies like 432 or 528. I do not need to understand the science behind them to know how they affect me. I feel it almost immediately. The tension in my head relaxes, my breath slows down, and my heart rate follows. I have come to love those times, when I can drop my shoulders and monitor my thoughts and just sit in peace. That is heaven to me.

Sometimes I listen to crown chakra singing bowls. There is something about those sounds that feels like a reset. The sound resonates all though my body, relaxing every nerve. It feels like someone gently pressing a button inside me that says, "You are safe. You can slow down now, you can breath."

I do just that, while the beautiful sound is playing, I breathe, deeply and intentionally. In through my nose. Out through my mouth, again and again. I focus on slowing my breath because I know that when I slow my breath, my body follows. My nervous system listens and all my emotions settle right on down. You should definitely try it.

Breathing is the ritual I return to the most because it always works. Breath is life, without it we die. Not sure why breath work is not taught to children in America. In my travels to other countries I found that many other countries know the importance of the breath. Some call it Prana, Breath of Life. I think it should be taught in pre-school. We could truly have a better world if children that young were taught the importance of breath and regulating their emotions.

I have done enough inner work that I am no longer reactive the way I once was. I do not explode when someone upsets me. I do not lash out or lose control anymore. But that does not mean my body does not feel things. If one of my children does something that upsets me, I might feel my head tighten. My chest might constrict or my stomach might knot up. The reaction may not come out of my mouth, but it shows up in my body.

That is when ritual steps in. It's time to breathe. We all breathe unconsciously and by default daily but what I mean is intentional controlled breathing. Sometimes it is monitoring my breathing that works for me. Other times it may be gospel music. There are certain songs that lift me up instantly. That music has carried me through some of the heaviest moments of my life. It reminds me of where I come from and what I have lived through.

For some people, church itself is a ritual. Sitting in a sanctuary and hearing the word of God may do it for them. Feeling the energy of collective worship may inspire them. Letting the music move through you. There is no one right ritual. There is only what works for you. Create daily rituals that make you feel good about yourself and life.

Walking is one of my rituals. Sometimes just moving my body in Zumba class makes me feel great. Running is a ritual for many people. They may love the rhythm, or release of toxins from their that they get from sweating. Even sitting quietly and doing absolutely nothing on purpose can be a ritual if it brings you back to your peaceful, happy self.

What matters is not what the ritual looks like. What is

important is that you have one for yourself. Daily rituals are how you prevent imbalance from becoming burnout. It is how you stop stress from living permanently in your body.

The mistake many people make is waiting until they are overwhelmed to take care of themselves. Building positive, productive rituals works best when it is proactive, not reactive. When you build it into your life as maintenance instead of emergency repair.

I do not wait until I am completely unraveling to breathe or to sit outside in the sun. I don't wait until I am exhausted to slow my life down. Nor do I wait until my body is screaming from fatigue and exhaustion for me to finally listen to it. That is something I learned through experience, and it is a lesson I want to pass on to you. It will definitely change your life for the better.

Your body is always communicating with you. Through fatigue, irritability, anxiety etc. Ritual is how you respond instead of ignoring those signals.

Balance is not about eliminating stress. Stress is part of life. Balance is about knowing how to bring yourself back to center when stress shows up. It is about not allowing yourself to become overwhelmed. You are not weak for needing to create positive rituals to keep yourself balanced, you are wise.

When you take time to breathe, to listen to music that soothes you, to walk, to pray, to sit in stillness, to reset your mind, you are telling your nervous system that it does not have to stay in fight mode. You are teaching your body that safety exists even when life is demanding.

That is powerful! I have built businesses and raised children. I have navigated grief, pressure, and responsibility. I did not do those things by ignoring my inner world. I did them by learning how to regulate myself so I could continue without losing myself to the pressures of life.

Daily rituals are not frivolous indulgences. They are tools, positive tools that help to anchor you. They are how you show up for your life without sacrificing your health, your peace, or your spirit.

You do not need to adopt my rituals exactly. You need to discover your own. Design ones that calm and center you. Create ones restore you and bring you joy, and remind you who you are when the noise gets loud.

Once you find them, you return to them daily. Make them part of your daily life. Not because your life is falling apart, but because you are committed to staying balanced while you build, create, love, and live.

That is how alignment becomes a lifestyle, not just an idea.

9

Everyday Alignment

Balance is not something you arrive at once and keep forever. It isn't a destination you check into and unpack at. It is a practice and a daily choice. It is a learned behavior that anyone can achieve. It is a way of moving through your life with awareness instead of being on autopilot. Alignment is not reserved for meditation retreats, mountaintop moments, or quiet seasons where nothing is demanded of you. Alignment is meant to be lived in real time, in real life, while you are working, building, parenting, healing, loving, and living your life.

 Googles definition of **Spiritual Alignment** is: a state of harmony where your actions, values and inner self are consistent with perceived higher truth, divine will, or your authentic purpose, often involving a connection to a God source energy or universal consciousness, leading to inner peace, authenticity and effortless flow in life. It is about aligning your mind, heart and actions with your deepest belief or a greater cosmic order, moving be beyond ego and worldly concerns.

 Everyday alignment is what happens when you begin to notice how you feel in your body, how you speak to yourself in your mind, and how you move through your day emotionally. It is the willingness to pause and ask yourself if the way you are living actually matches the way you want to feel. It is learning to recognize when something is off before it turns into burnout, resentment, illness, or emotional collapse.

For a long time, I believed alignment meant being calm. I believed it meant peace at all times. I thought it meant that once you reached a certain level of spiritual awareness, life would stop pulling at you from all directions. What I learned instead is that alignment does not remove the pressures of life. It teaches you how to respond to it. Alignment does not eliminate responsibility. It teaches you how to carry it without losing yourself.

Everyday alignment starts with honesty. Honest awareness of where you are overextending yourself. Being honest about how you are truly feeling inside? It begins with acknowledgment of where you are ignoring your own needs. it is checking in with yourself mentally and emotionally. Also recognizing when your body is saying no while your mouth keeps saying yes. You cannot align what you refuse to look at. Balance requires the courage to be truthful with yourself without judgment. If you are feeling sad, depressed and frustrated you must stop and sit still, in complete silence and acknowledge your current state of mind.

There were seasons in my life where I was accomplishing incredible things while slowly disconnecting from myself. On the outside, I looked focused, driven, successful, and disciplined. On the inside, my nervous system was constantly on edge. My body and brain were tired. My mind was racing even when I tried to rest. I did not realize that imbalance does not always look chaotic. Sometimes it looks productive. Non-stop work, no sleep at all. That has most definitely been me on many occasion.

The practice of everyday alignment taught me that just because I can push through something does not mean I should. God designed our bodies to shut down at night for a reason. Just because I am capable does not mean it is sustainable. Even though I am strong does not mean I am meant to carry everything alone. Alignment taught me to listen before my body had to scream. I call it a crash and yea I have worked so hard for days straight that eventually my body would shut me down and I would be stuck in bed for two days. That is not balance, the is imbalance.

Alignment is the moment you choose to stop overriding your intuition and you stop negotiating with your exhaustion. It is the moment you stop explaining away your discomfort and listen to your body. Your body is not working against you. It is working for you. It speaks through tension, fatigue, anxiety, irritability, and restlessness long before it speaks through illness. There are always warning signs. Remember mind, body and soul work together. The body is the storehouse of our infinite spirit. The body can not be neglected. I think of my body as the beautiful wrapping paper for a magnificent, priceless gift.

The practice of learning to balance your mind and body is not about perfection. You will still get tired and frustrated. You will still feel overwhelmed at times, but you will develop tools to keep yourself in tune mentally, emotionally and spiritually. Alignment is not about eliminating those negative experiences. It is about responding to them with conscious awareness instead of punishment or reactive behavior. It is about learning how to support yourself instead of criticizing yourself for being human.

Everyday alignment means learning how to balance action with rest. Masculine energy with feminine energy. Doing with being. Pushing with receiving. Leading with allowing. Many of us were taught to value productivity more than presence. We were praised for how much we could handle, how much we could carry, how much we could sacrifice. Rarely were we taught how to listen to ourselves, how to slow down without feeling bad about it, or how to trust that rest is not laziness but wisdom.

There were times when I felt guilty for slowing down because I had so much to do. Clients waiting. I had a staff to manage and projects that were unfinished. What alignment taught me is that ignoring my body did not make me more effective. It made me exhausted and unfocused. It made me short tempered and it disconnected me from my creativity and clarity. Rest was never taking away from my work, but i did not believe that then. Getting more would have restored my ability to do it well.

Alignment also shows up in the way you speak to yourself. The tone of your inner dialogue matters more than most people realize. If your internal voice is harsh, critical, and impatient, no amount of external success will feel satisfying. Everyday alignment requires learning how to speak to yourself with the same compassion you offer others. It requires interrupting self judgment and replacing it with love.

One of the first steps in reversing these dis-empowering mental habits is first acknowledging exactly what you are saying to yourself that is not true. If what you are saying to yourself makes you feel bad internally, then more than likely it is not truth.

Take some time to identify exactly what you are saying to you about yourself. That is a key element is attaining balance in all areas of your life. These behaviors must first be identified before you can change them. You can't reverse negative self talk if you have not accepted that it is happening and that you have the ability to change it. Don't persecute and convict yourself for having negative inner dialogue. Being at a point in your life where you can admit and recognize this inner language puts you way ahead of your past self.

We do more internal damage to ourselves than anyone in our lives could ever do to us. I was guilty of this for many years. No matter what level of success I achieved, I maintained the voice in my head that told me I was not valuable. I was my own worst enemy.

Instead of asking what is wrong with me, alignment asks what is my mind and body trying to tell me. Instead of saying I should be able to handle this, alignment asks what support do I need right now. Instead of pushing through discomfort, alignment invites you to pause and listen to your internal dialog. You are the most important person in your world and hopefully this book will teach you to be kinder to yourself.

The journey towards balance extends into how you set boundaries. Alignment teaches you that boundaries are not walls meant to keep people out. They are structures that protect your energy so you can show up fully where you are meant to be. Saying no is not rejection. It is redirection. It is choosing yourself without abandoning others. There were several draining family relationships that I had to step back from so that I could work on myself. They were not happy about it but they were takers and I am a giver. Unbalanced relationships like that are draining.

There was a time when I believed being available for everyone meant being loving. I believed saying yes meant being kind. But when I look back I realize I simply allowed a lot of people to use me. What alignment taught me is that resentment festers where boundaries are missing. Burnout grows where self love and respect is ignored. You come first. You cannot stay spiritually balanced while constantly betraying your own needs.

Everyday alignment also asks you to become mindful of what you consume emotionally, mentally, and spiritually. The conversations you engage in. The environments you remain in. The media you absorb. The people you allow access to your inner world. Not everything deserves your energy. Not everyone deserves your emotional labor. There were two specific female friends that I had to eliminate from my life in order to sustain my spiritual growth. They were toxic energy vampire and I so am glad I had the strength to cut them off.

Another form of alignment is choosing peace over proving a point. The Leo in me used to be extremely stubborn about backing down if I felt I was right. When you evolve you find that, those things do not even matter. You easily let it go before provoking chaos over proving your point. Your peace becomes your priority, and it becomes easier to walk away from situations that drain you even if they once felt familiar. Growth often requires releasing negative patterns that kept you safe in earlier seasons but now keep you stuck.

One of the most powerful aspects of everyday alignment is learning how to return to yourself quickly. Life will still throw unexpected challenges at you. People will still disappoint you. Plans will still change and life will still challenge you. Alignment does not prevent disruption. It shortens the recovery time. It allows you the ability to reset and recalibrate instead of spiral out of control.

You begin to notice when you are off center sooner. You identify your and you stop ignoring the signs. You are able to return a place of love and calm using whichever tools work for you.to your body. This is how life is supposed to be, you steering your own ship and becoming the master of your own fate.

Balance is not about floating above everyday life. It is about standing firmly within it. It is about being grounded while still being open and progressive. Being strong while still being soft or being disciplined while still being gentle.

The practice of everyday alignment is how you turn spiritual understanding into lived experience. It is how you bring balance out of books and into your everyday reality. It is how you stop compartmentalizing your spirituality and start integrating it into your daily decisions, your relationships and your work life.

Alignment is not something you earn. It is something you choose again and again daily. Some days you will choose it easily and other days you will forget and have to begin again. There is no failure in that. There is only practice. and advancement towards your purpose. The more you practice, the more natural it becomes. You begin living in a way that feels honest, sustainable, and deeply connected to source.

I am excited for you, your life is what you make of it.

10

Returning to My True Nature

One of the biggest misconceptions about spiritual growth is the idea that once you find peace, you keep it forever. Some feel that once you do the work, learn the tools, pray the prayers, and discipline your thoughts, life somehow stops testing you. I wish that were true, but it isn't. What spiritual growth actually gives you is not immunity from pain, but the ability to return to center when pain shows up.

Life will always show up. Life will keep life-ing as they say today. I have had to return to center more times than I can count. Even on my path of peace. Even with the tools I had learned and the years of inner work behind me. Being centered is not a destination. It is a practice that you come back to again and again, sometimes daily, sometimes hourly but it can be a new way of life.

There were two moments in my life that tested everything I believed in. All I taught myself, all the self-help books I read and wrote, and positive rituals I created, almost went right out of the window.

There were two life altering moments where the ground

disappeared beneath me and I had no choice but to either apply what I knew or completely unravel. On two separate occasions, two of my adult children went missing. One of them was missing for three days, and the other for three weeks. It almost killed me. There are no words that fully capture what that does to a mother's heart.

When your child is young, your fear is physical. You can see them and can touch them. You can intervene if you see danger coming. But when your child is grown and out in the world making their own choices, fear becomes psychological. It becomes imagined. Your mind fills in every blank with the worst possible outcome. You picture scenes you never wanted to see. You imagine endings you cannot survive.

I thought it was going to literally kill me. I truly did. But it didn't, and the reason it didn't is because I returned to center. I called on all those tools and positive rituals. I had to, or I would have died there emotionally, mentally, spiritually. But I couldn't do that. I still had other children to raise. I still had life asking me to show up. I had a responsibility to myself. I had to go within and do more spiritual work than I had done that far. I had to cast out negative images and replace them with positive ones. I had to return to center.

Returning to center in moments like that is not peaceful or pretty. It is deliberate and necessary. It is a learned disciplined that can calm your spirit. It is sometimes the hardest thing you will ever do.

I had to call on everything I believed in. Everything I had studied and practiced. All the peaceful ritualistic work like meditation, affirmations and breath work. I had written about all of these thing in my books. I had urged others to use these tool and now my feet were being held to the fire.

I had to actively remove images from my mind and monitor every single thought. Images of my child hurt. Images of my child dead somewhere. horrible thoughts of tragedy that my imagination offered me over and over again. Those images came uninvited, and I had to refuse them every single time. I teach this to some of my Life-Coaching students. I had to Catch the thought and Cast it out. Catch and Cast repeatedly. It is a system that works.

That is what returning to center looks like when it matters. It is not pretending you are okay. It is not bypassing pain or denying fear. It is choosing, again and again, not to live inside it. I prayed intentionally and effectively. Not desperation and panic. But with clearly defined intention.With authority, speaking and claiming with my mouth that my children were OK. I reminded myself who God is to me and the unshakable faith I had in our Divine source. I reminded myself who I am and stood strong on my beliefs. Just because I can picture something does not mean it is happening. I refused to allow those images to debilitate me.

I sat in silence. A lot. People underestimate silence because some think it does not feel productive. But silence is where you regain control of your mind. It is where you hear your own thoughts clearly enough to interrupt them. Silence is where you notice when fear is trying to hijack your body. It was in that silence that I learned something even deeper. Stillness itself is a doorway back to center. When I say '' Center Yourself" I mean re-aligning yourself with your faith and beliefs. Merging with the amazing divine source that I choose to call God and commanding the best outcome. Not sinking into a mental and emotional pit of death and destruction.

Stillness is one of the most powerful tools we have, and it is one of the least taught. In American culture, we are taught to get up and do, to fix it now, to push on, to talk it through, to stay busy. Silence makes people uncomfortable but it is truly a gift. Stillness is often mistaken for laziness or avoidance. Meditation is sometimes viewed as strange or unnecessary.

I have been fortunate enough to have had several opportunities to travel to other countries. When you travel, you see something very different. In places like Peru, Istanbul, Egypt, and Greece, meditation is not exotic. It is normal, natural behavior that is respected. It is woven into daily life. People sit and breathe. They close their eyes and honor God in their own way. They honor the inner world as much as the outer one. They dedicate time to cultivating their spiritual life.

I was able to go inside of the sacred Kings Chamber in the Giza Pyramids and chant with my spiritual group. The energy felt in there was unlike anything I have every felt in my life. I have been inside the Temple of Isis in Cairo and placed my personal healing crystals on the sacred alter. It was a life changing experience. It was also proof that there is a powerful unseen energy and that is with us always.

It is still my dream to go to Tibet one day and take my daughters with me. To sit in that beautiful spiritual energy. To experience a culture that understands that stillness is not empty. It is full. It is balance.

Meditation is one of the most direct ways to return to center. Not because it erases problems, but because it reconnects you to yourself beneath them. When you meditate, you are not trying to stop your thoughts. Thoughts will come no matter what you do. Memories will always surface. Meditation teaches you how to observe without drowning. It teaches you that you are not your thoughts. You are the one witnessing them. I love the art of meditation and I pray it becomes more accepted and valued in the United States.

For people who have lived through trauma, stillness can feel intimidating at first. Closing your eyes can bring things up, and that silence can feel loud and uncomfortable. That is why meditation is not something you force. It is something you gently build a relationship with.

There are many forms of meditation. Guided meditation. Transcendental meditation. Sound meditation with singing bowls or frequencies which I am very familiar with. I began offering sound meditation in my studio in 2025 (#SoundWith-SaBrina).. Even sitting quietly with just your breath. The form does not matter. The intention does.

When I meditate, I am not escaping life. I am remembering myself and the divine being that I am. I am stepping out of reaction and into awareness.

I love grounding as well. Grounding works the same way, but through the body. Sometimes my daughter and I go into our backyard and place our bare feet on the grass. No phones. Not a lot of talking. Just pure connection to the earth. We know there are healing properties in the earth. The earth stabilizes and clams the body. It balances us.

Mother Earth is our friend. She is working in our favor. In Peru that call her Pachamama. I travel to ancient places like Machu Picchu. My spiritual group and i were able to take off our shoes and put bare feet on the ancient ancestral grounds. Grounding brings scattered energy down into the body. It pulls you out of your head and back into the present moment. It reminds you where you come from.

Meditation connects you inward and upward. Grounding connects you downward and outward. Together, they create balance.

Once I learned to ground myself through stillness and breath work, I could continue in the midst of the storm. there is no greater storm that your children being missing. I listened to binaural beats constantly during those times. Constantly. They helped regulate my nervous system when my emotions threatened to overwhelm me. They slowed my breath and steadied my heart. They reminded my body that it did not need to stay in panic mode.

But silence remained my anchor. Being a parent to adult children is one of the greatest spiritual tests there is. You cannot protect them the way you once did. You cannot swoop them up and keep them safe. You have to trust what you poured into them, and that trust is terrifying.

I know many parents understand exactly what I'm talking about. The awareness that life can happen to your children when you are not there to intervene. The fear that quietly sits beneath your joy.

I had to make a decision. I could live in fear, or I could live in faith. I could imagine everything that could go wrong, or I could return to center and anchor myself in what is.

Fear does not protect your children. It only steals your peace. So I chose center. Again and again.

I breathed and I prayed. I sat in silence for hours. I monitored my thoughts, I grounded myself. That is how I mentally survived those trying times. That is what balance looks like in real life. One of my children was located the other is still missing to this day. God Bless you Justin, I will love you forever.

If you are reading this and you have been through something that knocked you off center, something that you did not think you could recover from. I want you to know this. You are not broken because it hurts. Nor are you weak because you struggled to be optimistic. You are human. What matters is not how many times you lose your center. What matters is that you know how to return to it.

Balance is not something we achieve once and keep forever. It is something we practice, sometimes daily, sometimes moment by moment. Life will pull you out of alignment. Loss will shake you. Love will test you. Responsibility will stretch you. Fear will visit many times. That does not mean you have failed. It means you are alive. Balance is not the absence of struggle. It is the ability to steady yourself in the middle of it.

Throughout this book, I have talked about balance in many forms because balance is not one-dimensional. It lives in how we think, how we feel, how we eat, how we rest, how we love, and how we respond when life does not go according to plan. It lives in the relationship between action and rest, logic and intuition, discipline and compassion. It lives in the harmony between masculine energy that moves, protects, and builds, and feminine energy that nurtures, feels, and restores. When one dominates without the other, we suffer. When they work together, we heal.

Balance teaches us when to push forward and when to pause. It teaches us that strength does not always look like force, and softness does not mean weakness. It reminds us that nourishment is not only about food, but about what we consume emotionally, mentally, and spiritually. What we allow into our minds, what we hold in our bodies, and what we tolerate in our relationships all affect our sense of peace.

Returning to your true nature does not mean becoming someone new. It means remembering who you were before life taught you to brace, to armor, to overextend, or to shut down. It means learning how to listen to yourself again. It means honoring your needs without guilt and setting boundaries without apology. It means choosing awareness over reaction and alignment over chaos.

Balance is not found outside of you. It is cultivated within you. It is the quiet decision to come back to center when fear tries to pull you into the future or pain tries to drag you into the past. It is choosing presence over panic. It is learning to trust yourself enough to sit with discomfort without being consumed by it.

If there is one thing I hope you take from this book, it is this. You are not meant to live at the extremes. You are not meant to be hardened by life or dissolved by it. You are meant to live in harmony with yourself. You are meant to feel deeply without drowning. You are meant to stand strong without becoming rigid. You are meant to live fully without losing yourself.

Balance is not perfection. It is awareness and compassion. It is the practice of returning to what is true when everything else feels uncertain. That is why we need it.

This is not the end of your journey. It is an invitation to live it with intention, presence, and grace. Return to yourself as often as you need to. Your center is always there, waiting for you to return to it.

Egypt 2018

Machu Picchu 2017

My son and I in 2016

Placing our healing crystal and jewelry on the sacred alter in the Temple of Isis, Egypt

About the Author

SaBrina Fisher Reece was once known throughout California as "The Braid Queen." For more than twenty-six years, she owned and operated the legendary Braids By SaBrina, a celebrated salon and school on Adams Boulevard in Los Angeles. It grew into the largest and most influential braiding establishment in the city, where artistry, empowerment, discipline, and community came together in powerful ways. Her success was entirely self-made, built through perseverance, resilience, and vision, often without consistent external support or validation.

As she stepped into the second half of her life, SaBrina felt a deeper calling unfolding within her. The story behind her success was not just one of entrepreneurship, but one of faith, healing, self-trust, and spiritual awakening. Early experiences of abandonment and profound personal loss led her inward, where she began the real work of emotional healing and inner mastery. What started as creative expression evolved into purposeful transformation.

Today, SaBrina writes self-help books rooted in emotional healing, personal growth, and spiritual awareness. Blending lived experience with motivational insight and metaphysical understanding, she explores themes of balance, resilience, self-mastery, and the unseen forces that shape human thought and behavior. Through her writing and motivational speaking, she guides readers toward deeper self-awareness, renewed confidence, and lives that feel intentional and aligned from the inside out.

She is the author of numerous self-help and transformational works, including *My Spiritual Smile, Kicking Depression In the Butt, Your Mind Is Magic, Perfectly Positive, Living Life on a Higher Frequency, Spiritual Balance, Angry World, Become Your Own Cheerleader*, God is Not a Man: Rediscovering the Divine Balance of Masculine and Feminine Within Us All, *Self Sabotage, How to Get Exactly What You Want From God, When I Say "I Am"*, and the popular Ebooks: *Imagine: Learn How to Use Your Imagination to Design the Life You Desire, You're Not Religious -You're Spiritual-I Get It: Bridging the Gap Between the Two*, , *Take A Breath With Bri: The Power of Intentional Breathing, Is This Why They Burned The Books?: Buried Wisdom From The Past*.

Her passion for sound and frequency has led her to explore the healing power of crystal sound bowls, tuning forks, and flow chimes, tools designed to help harmonize the body, mind, and spirit. Now residing in the enchanting landscapes of New Mexico, "The Land of Enchantment," she offers Sound Vibration Sessions that invite others to slow down, breathe deeply, and reconnect with their higher selves. While she embraces these modalities, she reminds her students and readers that there is no single path to peace. Every journey is sacred, and every sincere method of connecting with the Divine carries value.

Above all, SaBrina is a devoted mother of four, Justin, Joi, Jayden, and Journey, and a proud grandmother to Raiden Jesse and Rio Jordan. Watching them, and those she teaches, awaken to their divine potential remains her greatest joy.

Her message is simple and enduring: we are each born with divine energy, a God-given power to create, to heal, and to live fully. The goal is not perfection, but peace. The journey is not to escape life, but to embrace it, to use positive tools to take control of the mind and become the master of your fate.

You can connect with me on:
- https://in59secondspublishing.com
- https://www.facebook.com/BraidQueenSaBrinaReece

Also by SaBrina Fisher Reece

SaBrina Fisher Reece writes self-help books rooted in emotional healing, personal growth, and spiritual awareness. Her work blends lived experience with motivational insight, often exploring themes of balance, resilience, self-mastery, and the unseen forces that shape our thoughts and behaviors. Drawing from both practical reflection and metaphysical concepts, her writing encourages readers to develop greater self-awareness, reconnect with their inner strength, and create more intentional, aligned lives...

How to Get Exactly What You Want From God:

How to Get Exactly What You Want From God: Mastering the Art of Effective prayer: shows you how to pray with results. Inside, you'll learn how to make specific requests, build the faith needed to sustain them, and match your thoughts and emotions to the outcome you want. SaBrina teaches you how to interrupt negative self-talk, eliminate doubt, and step into a mindset that attracts divine answers quickly and clearly. This is your guide to intentional prayer, spiritual alignment, and receiving blessings without hesitation.

What if prayer was never meant to be begging, pleading or waiting in doubt – but instead a powerful alignment with what God has already promised you?

In this amazing book *SaBrina Fisher Reece* dismantles the myths around ineffective prayer and exposes the spiritual authority each believer already possesses. Blending deep spiritual wisdom, real life testimonies of divine intervention, and the practical mindset of a seasoned entrepreneur. SaBrina teaches readers how to pray with confidence, clarity, gratitude and expectation, so they can finally see there hearts desires appear in real time.

Through powerful personal stories of protection, provision, survival and miraculous alignment, SaBrina reveals that prayer becomes effective when belief replaces fear and faith replaces uncertainty. The Kingdom of Heaven is already within you. This book is not about religion as routine – it is about relationship, authority and conscious co-creation with God.

In this book you will learn:

- Eliminate doubt from your prayer
- Speak with spiritual authority and conscious intention
- Align your thoughts, emotions and actions with your prayers
- Recognize Divine intervention in your life
- Trust God's timing without losing hope

This is not a book about hoping and wishing.

This is a book about knowing and trusting that "It Already Done!"

Effective prayer doesn't wonder if God will move - it prepares your life for when He does

PROFOUND
ntroduction to the Profound Series

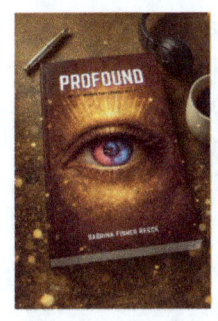

This series was not written to convince you of anything.

It was written to remind you of something.

For most of my life, I searched for answers the same way many people do. I looked outward. I prayed, studied, worked, endured, and tried to become better by force. I believed growth meant effort alone and that transformation required suffering. I was taught, as many of us are, what to believe, what to question, and what to avoid.

What I did not realize at the time was that I was not missing faith.

I was missing understanding.

The *Profound Series* was born from a deeply personal journey of self-discovery, healing, and expansion. It is the result of decades of reading ancient texts, studying metaphysical teachings, reflecting on spiritual principles, and most importantly, applying this wisdom in real life. This series is not meant to replace religion, tradition, or belief systems. It is meant to widen the lens.

Religion offers structure, community, and devotion. Ancient wisdom offers context, depth, and responsibility. Together, they reveal something powerful: that you are not separate from the divine, and you were never meant to live disconnected from your inner power.

This series exists because I discovered that much of what we are seeking has already been known for centuries. Long before modern psychology, neuroscience, or self-help, ancient philosophers, mystics, teachers, and spiritual scholars understood the relationship between thought, emotion, consciousness, and reality. They understood that the mind is creative, that belief shapes experience, and that life responds to awareness.

The first book, **Profound**, is about remembering. It is about gathering ancient wisdom and recognizing truths that may feel familiar even if you are encountering them for the first time. This is the awakening stage. The moment when something inside you says, "There is more."

The second book, **Activate**, is about embodiment. Knowledge alone does not change a life. It must be practiced. This book moves wisdom from the intellect into daily living. It teaches you how to tap into the divine energy within you and apply what you have learned in practical, grounded ways.

The third book, **Think**, is about mastery of the mind. Thought is not passive. It is creative. This book guides you in becoming aware of your inner dialogue, understanding how thoughts shape experience, and learning how to consciously direct the mental patterns that influence your life.

The fourth book, **Live**, is about integration. This is where knowledge, practice, and awareness become who you are. You no longer strive to be aligned. You live aligned. You move through the world with clarity, compassion, and confidence, embodying the wisdom you have gained.

Together, these four books form a complete journey.

Awakening. Activation. Mastery. Expression.

This is not a quick fix. It is not spiritual bypassing. It is not about perfection. It is about responsibility. Responsibility for your thoughts. Responsibility for your emotional state. Responsibility for the energy you bring into the world.

The world does not need more information. It needs more

conscious people. People who are self-aware. People who understand cause and effect at the level of thought and emotion. People who can pause, reflect, and respond instead of react. People who live from inner alignment rather than fear.

You were never meant to live small, disconnected, or powerless. You were meant to participate in your own evolution.

This series is an invitation. Not to abandon what you believe, but to expand it. Not to follow me, but to follow your own inner knowing. Not to search endlessly outside yourself, but to reconnect with what has always been within you.

If you are reading this, you are ready.

Ready to remember.

Ready to activate.

Ready to master your mind.

Ready to live fully.

Welcome to the journey.

Kicking Depression in the Butt i

Kicking Depression in the Butt is a raw, faith-infused, and deeply practical guide for anyone who is tired of surviving in silence and ready to reclaim their life.

Drawing from her own lived experiences with trauma, abandonment, loss, and depression, SaBrina Fisher Reece invites readers into an honest conversation about what depression really feels like, and how to fight back. This book does not minimize pain or offer shallow positivity. Instead, it helps readers recognize depression as an internal enemy, interrupt destructive thought cycles, and rebuild their inner world with intention, truth, and daily tools that actually work.

Through personal storytelling, spiritual insight, and mindset-shifting strategies, SaBrina shows readers how to stop identifying with their darkest thoughts and begin designing a life that protects their peace. She addresses the realities of trauma, triggers, boundaries, faith, therapy, medication, and personal responsibility, offering a balanced approach that honors both professional support and inner work.

Kicking Depression in the Butt is for the person who keeps showing up while quietly falling apart. It is for those who smile while suffering, who feel strong on the outside but exhausted on the inside. Most of all, it is a reminder that depression may visit, but it does not get to stay, and it does not get to become your identity.

This book is not about perfection. It's about progress. It's about learning how to fight for your mind, your peace, and your future, one thought, one choice, and one day at a time.

Because as long as you have breath in your body, your story is not over, and you still have the power to kick depression in the butt.

UNBROKEN

Unbroken: Mending the Holes Left by Life is a self-help and personal growth book that explores emotional healing after trauma, abandonment, and loss. Drawing from lived experience and spiritual insight, SaBrina Fisher Reece introduces the concept of "holes" formed by unresolved pain and explains how these wounds influence thoughts, behaviors, and relationships.

This book guides readers toward greater self-awareness, emotional balance, and inner healing by addressing the mind's role in recovery and the importance of compassion, forgiveness, and intentional thought patterns. *Unbroken* offers a reflective and empowering approach to healing, helping readers understand their past without being controlled by it.

Designed for individuals seeking emotional growth and spiritual grounding, *Unbroken* provides insight into reclaiming wholeness and learning how to live with strength, clarity, and self-love after life's most difficult experiences.

Pressure Down Plates: Delicious Meals for Lower Blood Pressure

High blood pressure does not mean giving up flavor.

It does not mean bland food, boring meals, or feeling restricted at the dinner table. It means learning how to cook smarter, season differently, and nourish your body in a way that supports your heart.

In *Pressure Down Plates*, you will discover delicious, satisfying meals designed to help lower blood pressure naturally-without sacrificing taste. This cookbook focuses on simple ingredients, practical swaps, and flavorful combinations that make heart-healthy eating feel enjoyable instead of overwhelming.

Inside you'll find:

Low-sodium meals packed with flavor

Smart seasoning alternatives that don't rely on excess salt

Simple recipes for busy weeknights

Wholesome ingredients that support heart health

Easy dishes the whole family will love

Whether you are newly diagnosed, managing long-term hypertension, or simply wanting to be proactive about your health, this book gives you meals you can actually look forward to eating.

Taking care of your heart should feel empowering-not limiting.

Lower the pressure. Lift your plates. Enjoy your food again.

Mind Is All

In Mind Is All: Manipulating Ideas in a New Direction, SaBrina Fisher Reece explores the mechanics of thought-how ideas form, how they gain power, and how they quietly shape decisions, behavior, and belief. This book focuses less on positivity as a concept and more on mental leadership: learning how to consciously guide thought before it guides you.

Rather than motivating through inspiration alone, this book challenges readers to examine where their attention goes and why. It offers a framework for recognizing habitual thinking and deliberately steering it in a new, more constructive direction.

In this book, you'll learn how to:
   Identify ideas that limit your growth
   Redirect mental momentum instead of fighting it
   Strengthen focus and internal discipline
   Replace unconscious reactions with intentional thought
   Use awareness to influence outcomes and decisions

Mind Is All is about reclaiming authority over your inner world. When you learn how ideas are formed and sustained, you gain the ability to reshape them-and in doing so, reshape your experience of life.

This book is for readers ready to think differently, not just feel better.

God is Not a Man

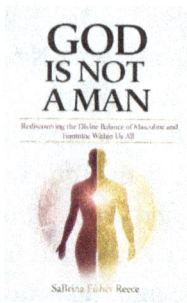

Is God exclusively male, or have we limited the image of the divine through tradition and culture?

In *God Is Not a Man: Rediscovering the Divine Balance of Masculine and Feminine Within Us All*, SaBrina Fisher Reece explores a powerful and often overlooked truth: divine source is not confined to gender. Drawing from scripture, ancient wisdom, global spiritual traditions, personal travel experiences, and modern psychological insight, this book challenges inherited assumptions while honoring faith.

Reece takes readers on a journey through Egypt, Greece, Indonesia, and Peru in search of a deeper understanding of God. Along the way, she examines universal law, the balance of masculine and feminine energy, and the spiritual maturity required to hold faith without limiting it. With clarity and conviction, she reveals how imbalance in our understanding of divine image has shaped theology, identity, and culture.

This book offers healing for women who have felt spiritually secondary and freedom for men who have felt pressured to suppress emotional depth. It speaks to the seeker who longs for truth without abandoning reverence. It affirms that strength and tenderness, authority and compassion, structure and intuition are not opposites but complementary expressions of one infinite source.

Rather than rejecting tradition, *God Is Not a Man* expands it. Rather than attacking faith, it deepens it. Readers will come away empowered, grounded, and more comfortable in their own wholeness, understanding that divine image is far greater than any single label.

For those ready to move beyond limitation and into balance, this book offers clarity, humility, and spiritual confidence.

How to Make More and Work Less
A Guide to Increasing Your Income Quickly is not another hustle book filled with recycled advice or unrealistic promises. It is a grounded, compassionate guide for people who have worked hard, played by the rules, and still found themselves facing financial uncertainty in a changing economy.

Written from lived experience, this book speaks directly to adults who are tired of surviving and ready to build a life that includes peace, stability, and abundance. With honesty and warmth, Bri Reece shows readers how to stop trading endless hours for diminishing returns and start creating income through their existing skills, knowledge, and life experience.

Blending practical insight with heartfelt encouragement, this book explores how to turn what you already know into income, how old school marketing still works in a digital world, and how teaching, writing, and speaking can create leverage without burnout. Most importantly, it addresses the mindset shift required to move from constant stress to sustainable freedom, reminding readers that struggle may have been part of their journey, but it was never meant to be their forever.

This book is for anyone who has worried quietly about bills, felt overlooked by a changing economy, or wondered if it was too late to start again. It offers clarity, hope, and real options for making more money while reclaiming time, dignity, and joy.

If you are ready to believe in possibility again and build a life that supports you instead of drains you, this book meets you exactly where you are and gently shows you what is still possible.

www.ingramcontent.com/pod-product-compliance
Lightning Source LLC
LaVergne TN
LVHW021714080426
835510LV00010B/993